"On the afternoon of September 11, 2001, I received a phone call from Dr. Debbie Almontaser, then a student of mine in a principal preparation program. The Twin Towers had just fallen, her son in the National Guard was heading to Ground Zero to help with rescue efforts, and she was being called upon to lead. We discussed her courageous work as an educator—for years she had devoted her practice to building bridges between communities and forging conversations across faiths. Now, she feared, our country's political discourse would turn against her and her Muslim colleagues in education. Her powerful work at that time distinguished her as a thought leader and she was approved to open a new dual language school, the only one teaching in Arabic and English in New York City. Quickly, the school she opened was caught in the crosshairs of that same political discourse, ultimately forcing her to leave her school, step back, reflect, research, and write. The result is *Leading While Muslim*, a profile of 14 Muslim principals that provides an important treatise on education, on diversity, and on the undue burdens placed on leaders from marginalized groups in navigating the fraught and complex terrain of leading our nation's schools. *Leading While Muslim* is an important contribution to the literature on school leadership and a must-read for all interested in how educators from marginalized groups find strength in themselves so that they can continue to serve children and hopefully contribute to a more just world."—Sandra J. Stein, former chief executive officer, NYC Leadership Academy

"Not much has been written about the challenges that American Muslim principals face. As a school leader, Debbie Almontaser finally gives voice to a much needed educational community: Muslim school leaders. Within these pages, she discusses topics that are encountered every day by these American Muslim school leaders. Almontaser creates a clear and coherent framework for her argument and her writing is clear and a pleasure to read. Each chapter is grounded in research and contains valuable reflections. Her emphasis on these school leaders is an essential component toward bridging the educational norms in contemporary public schooling. This book is among the best written I have seen on this educational topic. Almontaser has a lifetime of experience in public school education, including as a school leader. Today, she is helping education leaders and lay leaders. As a result of her experiences, she provides guidance and inspiration to focus on encouraging community cultural practices in our schools."—Wafa Hozien, PhD, Educational Leadership Department, Central Michigan University

Leading While Muslim

6/26/19

Dear Arlene & Mike!
Let us rise and lead
together!

Dr. Debbie
Almontaser

Leading While Muslim

*The Experiences of American Muslim
Principals After 9/11*

Debbie Almontaser

ROWMAN & LITTLEFIELD
Lanham • Boulder • New York • London

Published by Rowman & Littlefield
An imprint of The Rowman & Littlefield Publishing Group, Inc.
4501 Forbes Boulevard, Suite 200, Lanham, Maryland 20706
www.rowman.com

Unit A, Whitacre Mews, 26-34 Stannary Street, London SE11 4AB

British Library Cataloguing in Publication Information Available

Library of Congress Cataloging-in-Publication Data Available

ISBN 9781475840964 (electronic) | ISBN 9781475840940 (cloth : alk. paper) | ISBN 9781475840957 (pbk. : alk. paper)

∞ ™ The paper used in this publication meets the minimum requirements of American National Standard for Information Sciences Permanence of Paper for Printed Library Materials, ANSI/NISO Z39.48-1992.

Printed in the United States of America

To all the American Muslim principals who serve in public education across the United States.

Your dedication and commitment to transforming the lives of inner city youth in public education has left me in awe. Your actions speak volumes about American Muslims' acting on their faith to serve humanity. No matter the challenges that you have faced as an American Muslim, you have persevered with great dignity and grace. You are an inspiration to me and to all the lives that you have touched in your communities, especially the children for whom you have served as role models. Thank you for your tireless service!

Contents

Foreword

Like many other ethnic and religious groups before them, immigrant Muslims (in contrast to African American Muslims who are the descendants of slaves) have come to America to build a better life and future. For some Muslims, America has offered the possibility of better employment, educational opportunities and training for hoped-for success back home, and political asylum for others who have fled authoritative and oppressive governments. America has both touted and been looked to as a land of opportunity, democratic freedoms, and civil liberties.

Like many ethnic Catholics and Jews, finding one's place in the Christian established American mosaic proved more challenging than expected. Despite the fact that America was founded and developed as a nation of immigrants, the new Muslim arrivals were often not embraced, but marginalized. As a result, many Muslims, like other immigrants before them, were seen as foreigners who didn't speak the language and/or had different cultural traditions and practices. In contrast to ethnic Catholic Europeans who were at least Christian even if not White Anglo-Saxon Protestants, Muslims practiced what many regarded as a foreign religion with different beliefs and cultural traditions.

Like other immigrants, many Muslims initially lived and socialized among themselves even when they were integrated into America's educational systems or jobs. In a country where many citizens know little about Islam and see the United States as a Christian country (for some a Judeo-Christian country), Islam was not seen as an Abrahamic faith, as it has been viewed by many scholars who, like some Muslims, have maintained that Islam is an Abrahamic faith, part of a Judeo-Christian-Islamic tradition.

Today, like other groups before them, Muslims have become integrated into the American mosaic: economically, educationally, socially, professionally, and increasingly politically. Muslims are second to American Jews among faith communities whose followers are educated. Economically many are equal to non-Muslims in their economic livelihood. Professionally they span the economic spectrum with a large percentage of physicians, lawyers, engineers, and educators as well as blue-collar positions.

Yes, like other immigrant groups before them, in the past Muslims had gone through periods of marginalization and alienation, anti-Islam and anti-Muslim bias, discrimination and fearmongering, but it seemed manageable. All this would change dramatically on September 11, 2001.

9/11 AND ITS AFTERMATH

The 9/11 destruction of New York's World Trade Center and the attack on the Pentagon in Washington, DC, had an enormous impact on the safety, security, and civil liberties of America's Muslim population. Shortly after the attacks, we had a gathering of the Center for Muslim–Christian Understanding's international advisory board.

The legacy of the 9/11 and post-9/11 terrorist attacks served as an alarm that Osama Bin Laden and Al-Qaeda (AQ) were not just an international threat but also a domestic threat to the safety and security of the United States and Europe. However, too often media commentators, policy makers, political candidates, and hard-line Christian Zionists used that threat not simply to warn but to promote an exaggerated emphasis on the magnitude of the threat as was reflected in the rhetoric of presidential and congressional elections.

As a result, anti-Muslim rhetoric found a ready and compliant audience to their indiscriminate message that Islam and Muslims, rather than more specifically Muslim terrorists, were a domestic and international threat. From that point on, the vast majority of regular, law-abiding Muslims would be brushstroked by the actions of terrorists. Hostility and intolerance toward mainstream Islam and Muslims as well as their religious and cultural beliefs have threatened Muslim civil liberties and undermined the democratic fabric of America.

THE "MOSQUE AT GROUND ZERO"

Across the United States, a major debate erupted over building an Islamic community center a few blocks from the site of the World Trade Center. Politicians in the run-up to elections used fear of Islam as a political football. Newt Gingrich warned of the danger of Shariah taking over American courts. Rex Duncan of Oklahoma declared that there is a "war for the survival of

America," to keep the Shariah from creeping into the American court system. Even the new justice Kagan was being accused of being "Justice Shariah."

ISLAMOPHOBIA, MEDIA, AND PRESIDENTIAL ELECTIONS

By 2015, Islamophobia had grown exponentially and negative media coverage of Islam and Muslims had hit an all-time high. Domestic and international terrorist attacks (by AQ, ISIL [Islamic State of Iraq and the Levant]), mass and social media, and American presidential elections/politics have been major catalysts in the growth of Islamophobia. Fear of Islam and Muslims (not just militant extremists and terrorists) has become normalized in popular culture in America and in Europe.

According to the Public Religion Research Institute, "no religious, social, or racial and ethnic group [was] perceived as facing greater discrimination in the U.S. than Muslims" (Jones, Cox, Cooper, & Leinesch, 2015).

This in turn has had a significant impact on domestic policies that have threatened Muslim civil liberties, influenced the radicalization of Muslim and non-Muslim extremists, and informed and legitimated Western foreign policies: from invasion and occupation to drone attacks, U.S. and EU responses to the Arab Spring and Arab Winter, and U.S. and EU support for authoritarian allies.

American Elections

American political elections have been a major driver or trigger as seen in the 2008, 2012, and 2016 presidential and primary races. Donald Trump, the leading Republican candidate for president, advocated a temporary freeze on all foreign Muslim immigration, as well as the monitoring or even the forced closure of American mosques. The result? Trump soared in the polls.

When CNN's Anderson Cooper asked Trump if he thought "Islam is at war with the West," Trump responded: "I think Islam hates us. . . . There's tremendous hatred there. . . . We have to get to the bottom of it. There is an unbelievable hatred of us."

POST-9/11 AND MEDIA IMPACT ON POPULAR CULTURE

Mass media focus on explosive, headline events—"If it bleeds, it leads"—resulted in an imbalance in coverage and also provided a platform for anti-Islam and anti-Muslim statements in media by political leaders, media commentators, and a host of "preachers of hate." A comparison of 975,000 news stories from U.S. and European media outlets in 2001 versus 2011 demonstrated the shocking disparity of coverage. Networks significantly reduced

coverage on events in the Middle East and North Africa (MENA) and focused more on actions of Muslim militants.

In 2001, 2% of all news stories in Western media presented images of
Muslim militants, while just over 0.1% presented stories of ordinary Muslims. By 2011, 25% of the stories presented militant images, while 0.1%
presented images of ordinary Muslims.

The net result was an astonishing imbalance of coverage: a significant
increase in coverage of militants but no increase at all over the 10-year
period in the coverage of ordinary Muslims.

The anti-Islam and anti-Muslim messages promoted by Islamophobes and
their organizations and websites has brushstroked Islam and mainstream
American Muslims. The line between extremists and terrorists on the one
hand and mainstream Islam and Muslims on the other is often obscured or
even nonexistent. The result is an exaggerated fear about the magnitude of
the threat and attempts by those who see Islam as the culprit to engage in a
collective guilt and thus see Islam itself as a threat to America, leading to
calls for the monitoring of mosques, attempts to prevent mosque building or
to attack mosques and Muslims, and to see identifiers like the hijab worn by
many Muslim women as a dangerous sign.

While there has been a raft of literature on the above issues and problems,
it is only recently that there has been greater focus on the fallout from
Islamophobia and its impact on teachers and students in schools of Muslim
students, bullying by fellow students or teachers.

What we have not had is this important study produced by Dr. Debbie
Almontaser's book *Leading While Muslim: The Experiences of American
Muslim Principals After 9/11*, which fills a significant gap in our understand-
ing of the contexts in which many Muslim principals have functioned.
Through in-depth interviews and analysis of the experiences of these Muslim
educators, we see how the politicizing of fear and the negative image of
Islam and Muslims, perpetuated in popular culture, have negatively affected
Muslim principals in public schools.

One of the most stunning examples is the experience of the author, Dr.
Almontaser, detailed so thoroughly in this volume. Equally important are the
other cases presented that indicate the extent to which all too common issues
of hijab, having a Muslim name, or being perceived or cast as somehow
different and foreign and a potentially dangerous "Other" can undermine the
authority, effectiveness, and employment of principals or teachers. These
issues can make their jobs that much more difficult and engender a sense of
marginalization and alienation due to the actions of local government officials, school boards, and other teachers.

While Muslim religious identity does play a significant role in the job
performance of principals in public schools, unlike non-Muslim teachers,
their religion is often more emphasized rather than their skills and accom-

plishments by the influence of predominantly negative portrayals of Islam and Muslims in the political discourse and media. They are too often seen through the lens of stereotypes as different from their peers, as a foreign "Other" rather than their professional credentials, experiences, and track records.

The result, as Dr. Almontaser documents so effectively, is, in contrast to their non-Muslim colleagues, the pressures of a double standard and a climate of suspicion that requires an excessive cautiousness in what they say or do and political correctness. On the plus side, as a result of their experience, Muslim principals are often more aware of and responsive to minorities and the importance of a strong emphasis on diversity, tolerance, and civic engagement.

In an America that in a matter of decades will see a population that is largely Brown and not White and an Islam and Muslim population that is the second largest religious community, it is imperative that the lessons to be learned from *Leading While Muslim: The Experiences of American Muslim Principals After 9/11* be studied, taken seriously, and addressed.

—John L. Esposito
University Professor and Founding Director
Prince Alwaleed Bin Talal Center for Muslim–Christian Understanding
Director: The Bridge Initiative
ICC 260, Georgetown University

Preface

Over the years, the Muslim population has increased in size and social contribution. American Muslims hold a variety of professional careers in fields such as medicine, law, finance, and education. Muslim American women are one of the most highly educated groups, following Jewish American women. Muslim Americans have also earned salaries that afford them high standards of living. The pursuit of education in the Muslim American community is above the national average, with over 50% of Muslim Americans earning college and postgraduate degrees.

Today, schools in the United States are more diverse than they have ever been. According to the U.S. Census Bureau, the United States will become a majority–minority nation by 2044. Specifically, Whites will comprise 49.7% of the population, compared to Hispanics (25%), Blacks (12.7%), Asians (7.9%), and multiracial individuals (3.7%) (Frey, 2014). Such a prediction is largely due to the rapidly increasing number of Hispanic and Asian school-aged children born in the United States. However, while the diversity of the student body is important, the diversity of school leaders also warrants attention.

According to Phan, Hardesty, and Hug (2014), as of 2012, there were 89,530 public school principals. Of these, 71,920 were White; 9,070 Black non-Hispanic; 6,070 Hispanic of any race; and 2,470 were of other races and ethnicities. These other races and ethnicities include American Indian or Alaska Native, not Hispanic or Latino; Asian, not Hispanic or Latino; Native Hawaiian or Other Pacific Islander, not Hispanic or Latino; or two or more races, not Hispanic or Latino. As can be seen, the number of minority school leaders remains low.

Furthermore, these data do not capture the religious diversity of school leaders in the United States. The American Muslim community is very diverse, ranging from over 80 countries. Within the American Muslim community, the three largest groups are African Americans, South Asians, and Arabs. African Americans constitute the largest group, followed by South Asians from the Far East, and Arabs from the 22 Arab League nations, along with a growing number of Caucasian and Latino Americans.

Islam is the fastest growing religion in the world, and the estimates of the number of Muslims in the United States vary greatly. It is estimated that the population counts to approximately 3,480,000 in North America, while Moore (2009), three years prior, noted that there are approximately about 8 million in the United States and that this number continues to grow due to immigration and high birthrates within Muslim communities. And as noted, there are large numbers of Muslims in the United States who hold higher education degrees.

Throughout the course of Muslim history in the United States, the role and contribution of Muslims in the actual field of education has grown, despite the struggles due to political rhetoric. This book analyzes the lived experiences of school leaders particularly in a time when Muslims are living under great pressure.

AMERICAN MUSLIMS POST-9/11

In the aftermath of 9/11, there was backlash and discrimination against Arabs, Muslims, and South Asians, as well as government legislation, such as the Uniting and Strengthening America by Providing Appropriate Tools Required to Intercept and Obstruct Terrorism (USA PATRIOT) Act that have led to the detention and deportation of thousands of Muslims under the guise of the "war on terror."

The coverage of Islam and Muslims in the years after 9/11 has been continuous, along with the number of terrorist attacks committed by individuals who identify as Muslim. Government legislations and investigations completed under the war on terror have also been continuous.

Altheide (2006) examined how news reports about terrorism directly reflect the politics of fear geared to promote danger and to engender fear in audiences as a means to achieve political goals. His argument is drawn from his analysis of the use of terms such as *fear*, *crime*, and *terrorism* 18 months before and after the 9/11 attacks. His data reveal that not only was there an increase in the use of such terms but also that the use of the terms in news reports linked terrorism to crime and the term *victim*.

According to Altheide, the conflation of fear and terrorism through victimization since the 9/11 attacks is a strategic use of propaganda. The use of fear gives the audience the impression that, despite the normalcy of the state of affairs, there is an imminent crisis. Perversions of this fear not only influence popular culture but also affect people's capacity to experience and negotiate their everyday lives.

AMERICAN MUSLIM SCHOOL LEADERS

There has been a sizable amount of research on how 9/11 has had an impact on school communities, such as those comprising students, teachers, principals, and families of various racial and religious backgrounds, including Muslims. The presence of American Muslim principals remains minimal in public schools, in educational policy decision-making positions, and in district leadership. As such, research that has focused on American Muslim principals who serve in the public school system is lacking.

Although there is a body of research on American Muslim principals who serve in parochial Islamic schools, their experiences are very different. Thus, this study provides a voice for an underrepresented population of principals and fills a gap in the research.

This book examines the lived experiences of American Muslim principals who serve in public schools post-9/11 to determine whether global events, political discourse, and the media coverage of Islam and Muslims have affected their leadership and spirituality. The aim of the study is to allow researchers and educators to gain an understanding of the adversities that American Muslim principals have experienced post-9/11 and to determine how to address these adversities, particularly through decisions about educational policy and district leadership.

A total of 14 American Muslim school leaders who work in public schools post-9/11 across the United States participated in the study. The findings yielded six themes of political climate; role of the media; inferior and foreign: being seen as the "Other"; unconscious fear; spirituality; and education and communication over spectacle. Further, collective guilt and social responsibility emerged as two additional findings.

The research suggests that political spectacle and its effects have a large impact on the lives of American Muslim principals, particularly in regard to their leadership and spirituality. This will be illustrated through four case studies that touch on all of the findings.

It is the author's hope that the results of this study can be used to assist superintendents, school boards, human resource personnel, and other stakeholders to maximize their ability to select qualified candidates from an ethnically, racially, and religiously diverse pool of principals that includes American Muslims. The findings of this study are of value to school district leaders across the United States, universities, education advocacy groups, and American Muslim advocacy organizations and add to the existing knowledge base of minority studies in school leadership.

District leaders will gain an understanding of the adversities that American Muslim principals have experienced and can find ways to help educational policy and practice to address adversities. Further, based on the findings, universities can develop culturally sensitive teacher and administrator training programs to further encourage American Muslim educators to pursue school leadership positions. Advocacy groups and American Muslim organizations will be able to use the findings to improve policy.

AUTHOR'S EXPERIENCE

The author is the founding and former principal of the Khalil Gibran International Academy, the first Arabic dual language public school in the United States. The author herself was forced to resign as principal after a vitriolic attack by a small fringe group that did not want to see the school she founded, the Khalil Gibran International Academy, open because they felt it would propagate homegrown terrorism. In the weeks after the academy's announcement in the media, it experienced an onslaught of attacks as being a publicly funded *madrassah* to train homegrown terrorists. A *madrassah* can be defined as the Arabic word for "school," which has developed a negative connotation in a post-9/11 context.

Newspapers and news organizations, such as the *New York Sun*, the *New York Post*, *Fox News*, the blogosphere, and a small segment of the community launched a six-month attack on her and the school, which resulted in the author's forced resignation by the mayor of the city of New York and the New York City Schools chancellor. That was followed by an interview with the *New York Post*, in which her words were distorted and taken out of context.

Almontaser was forced out because the New York City Department of Education caved in to public and political pressures and used her defining of the word *intifada* with multiple perspectives and historical contexts as the linchpin to push her out. Her understanding of these events was confirmed by the Equal Employment Opportunity Commission (EEOC) in 2010 (Almontaser, 2012). As cited in the *New York Times*, the EEOC found that the Department of Education "succumbed to the very bias that creation of the school was intended to dispel and a small segment of the public succeeded in imposing its prejudices on D.O.E. as an employer" (Elliott, 2010).

The author has had a career spanning 25 years in the New York City Public School System, taught special education, trained teachers in literacy, and served as a multicultural specialist and diversity advisor. As an American Muslim of Yemeni heritage, she was raised and educated in the United States; she has served on panels related to Arab culture, Islam, cultural diversity, interfaith coalition building, and youth leadership at local, national, and international conferences.

Throughout her experience as an educator, she has been fortunate enough to be granted incredible opportunities that have allowed her to write and publish work on American Muslims and design curricula for Muslim studies projects at prestigious universities. Fostering cultural understanding and dialogue has been one of the author's greatest passions, and she has spent most of her life trying to contribute to this cause in whichever way she felt able.

In the days after 9/11, Almontaser was one among several American Muslims who worked to build bridges of understanding among New Yorkers through her educational work in schools and communities. She also became the voice for the families of Arab, Muslim, and South Asian New Yorkers whose family members were picked up in raids and detained and deported under the USA PATRIOT Act, which led her to be featured in local and international media outlets.

In 2005, based on her work as an Arab and Muslim educator in New York City, the author was recommended by the mayor's office and the New York City Department of Education to New Visions for Public Schools to establish a 6–12 high school that specializes in Arabic language and cultural studies. In 2006, after careful deliberation and an informal feasibility study to determine whether the timing was right for such a school, among interfaith clergy, elected officials, and community leaders, she put together a diverse design team and partnered with a nonprofit to start the process.

In February 2007, the Khalil Gibran International Academy was announced, with Almontaser as its founding principal. As an American Muslim principal who led a publicly funded Arabic dual language school in a post-9/11 world, she experienced firsthand being in the center of political spectacle that has caused her to question the role that her religion may have had in the debacle.

Throughout the course of the development of the school, there were times that she stated to the design team that a school that teaches Arabic may be seen as a threat and may face some opposition, but she never imagined that it would make international headlines and that her role as the principal would be seen as a threat, given her track record in education and advocacy work (Almontaser & Nevel, 2011).

The very purpose of the school she founded was to foster building bridges of understanding among students, staff, and the community at large through multicultural education. Her vision was to create a school that would offer students the opportunity to learn from curricula that are academically rigorous and culturally relevant, with hands-on experiences that allow students to go beyond "the four walls" to learn and to explore.

The author believed that the only way to overcome fear and misunderstanding is through education that allows individuals to learn about one another. She wanted to create a school that saw students of different ethnic, racial, and religious backgrounds as full human beings, who felt valued and celebrated by self and others. It is the genuine acceptance of one's differences that positively affects one's psychological well-being, personal relationships, and social consciousness.

In light of the experiences that she encountered, she became curious to know whether there were other American Muslim principals who may have had similar experiences and whether their leadership and spirituality as American Muslim principals had been affected. It was these questions that led her to develop this research project that focuses on the lived experiences of American Muslim principals in public schools. This is a segment of the American Muslim community that has yet to be studied. With an understanding of the author's experience, the purpose of this book, and points on American Muslims and education, readers can create a foundation for comprehending the necessity for this study.

Acknowledgments

I want to first acknowledge and thank my truly amazing husband Naji, who is my biggest cheerleader in the world. Without his words of encouragement and support over the last 30-plus years, I would not be where I am today. He has been my mountain of strength. I thank him from the bottom of my heart for all the sacrifices he has made for me throughout the course of my career. Naji, I love you with all my heart!

I want to thank my children, for their moral support throughout this journey! I want to thank my son-in-law, for all of his technology support! In addition, I thank my mother and two sisters for keeping me in their prayers!

I also want to acknowledge and extend my deepest gratitude to Dr. Carolyn Brown for pushing me to take on this topic and directing me to political spectacle theory as well as seeing me through my proposal defense on her deathbed. Her tireless commitment to her students will never be forgotten!

I also want to acknowledge and extend my deepest appreciation to Dr. Sheldon Marcus for making the transition from being one of my readers to becoming my mentor and helping me to complete this study. Thank you from the bottom of my heart. I also would like to extend a special thank-you to Dr. Kathleen Cashin and Dr. Carlos McCray for serving as my readers as well as Yusra Syed for her incredible editing skills.

Finally, to the dedicated 14 research participants, this study would not have become possible without you. Your willingness to do this was not only a service to this study but also to the American Muslim community globally. You have inspired me more than I can find the words to express. I look forward to what is in store for you as you continue to excel in public education!

Chapter One

Introduction

This book illustrates the lived experiences of 14 American Muslim school leaders in the post-9/11 world. Fourteen cases in the actual research are examined ranging from a number of ethnic and racial groups, male and female leaders, older and younger, working in larger and smaller urban communities, in a combination of elementary, middle, and high school levels in public and charter school settings. The findings of the research study will be shared along with four case studies to illustrate some of the challenges Muslim school leaders experience.

The following research questions were used to explore their lived experiences in this research:

1. How is the performance of American Muslim principals affected by their religion?
2. How do American Muslim principals perceive their treatment as compared to that of their non-Muslim colleagues in their district, in their relations with their staff, students, parents, and their school community at large?
3. How do American Muslim principals perceive that non-Muslims view them?
4. How are the challenges that American Muslim principals face different from those of their non-Muslim colleagues?
5. How is the spirituality of American Muslim principals affected by their leadership in a public school setting?

Many of these Muslim principals—including the author—have encountered some difficulties during times of heightened tensions locally, nationally, and globally. The year 2015 began with the *Charlie Hebdo* terror attacks in Paris and ended with the San Bernardino shooting. These events led to 71 mosque incidents that included vandalism, threats, desecration of Quranic texts, pig heads left outside entrances, targeting with bullets, and fire bombings, resulting in the highest ever recorded number of incidents [against Muslims], according to a Council on American–Islamic Relations (CAIR, 2015) report.

The 2016 presidential campaign had provided for a contentious climate on all sides of the spectrum. There was a growing debate on whether the campaigns had increased in speech on anti-Muslim rhetoric. Those who argued that such rhetoric did highlight Islamophobic tendencies pointed to the Republican Party front-runner Donald Trump calling for a "Muslim ban," and former candidate Ben Carson announcing that Muslims should not be permitted to become president (Bridge Initiative Team, 2015a).

Utilizing the above listed research questions as the primary framework, this book will address these main points and present its research in the following organization. What would further benefit readers would be a detailed understanding of the definition and meaning of leadership in the context of education. Chapter 2 will explore this discussion along with providing readers with a brief history of Jewish and Catholic experiences in education. Chapter 3 will explore the history of Muslims in America and their narrative in the current climate and education system, in the hopes of solidifying the foundation for understanding the study's goals.

Following a brief study of American Muslim history, Chapter 4 will delve into an explanation of how the study was conducted. The chapter will mention the research methodology, interview details with each subject, and the overall data collection process. At the conclusion of a comprehensive summarization of the entire study methodology, the book will then note the key findings of the research.

Chapter 5 will begin the research analysis by examining two of the key themes, political climate and the role of media. The chapter will explain how the general political climate plays a significant role in each of the principals' professional experience. Hand in hand with the present political climate, the role of the media in depicting Islam and the American Muslim experience also influences the experience of each research subject. Chapter 6 will continue off the previous chapter by noting more key themes that contribute to the experience of American Muslim principals, namely, being perceived as the "Other" or "inferior" and the internal development of an unconscious fear behavior.

Chapter 7 will examine the final key trend identified in this study, focused on the theme of spirituality. The chapter will discuss how each subject's experience as a principal has affected their spiritual growth and understanding of Islam. Chapter 8 will mention additional findings that were also present in the study, relating to positive experiences in which education and communication prevailed over fear and political spectacle with their colleagues and students. The chapter will also address notions of collective guilt and social responsibility emerging from the discussions with the interview subjects.

The final chapter will reflect on all the written reflections and data and shall attempt to answer each of the five initial research questions. Following the discourse on the research questions, the chapter will briefly note the limitations of the study and implications for future studies related to this subject area.

Chapter Two

The Meaning of Leadership

Having well-prepared principals at the helm of schools is an investment in creating positive school environments for both the faculty and the student body.

To better understand the lived experiences of American Muslim school leaders, a discussion of leadership is useful. International literature indicates that school leadership is at the center of school improvement and student outcomes (Walker & Riordan, 2010). Leadership in education is no different from leadership in other fields; it requires the same sense of purpose and value-driven action.

Challenges arise in education that must be received by a well-trained and qualified leader who is passionate about making a difference in the lives of students through positive influence. According to Creighton (1999), people who are motivated to have an impact on society through school leadership are driven by deep-rooted convictions. Moreover, schools are in dire need of leaders who are trained in quality leadership-preparation programs to ensure a positive impact on the school environment and to accomplish educational goals.

Ample research across a wide range of fields validates the claim that quality leadership is critical to the success of any organization (Kanji, 2008). This belief dates back many centuries. Blakney (1955) presents a view of an exemplary leader—Lao-Tzu, an ancient Chinese philosopher:

> He imparts instruction not through so many words but through a few deeds. He is a catalyst and though things would not get done as well if he were not there, when they succeed he takes no credit. And because he takes no credit, credit never leaves him.

Lao-Tzu believes that a leader who leads selflessly serves his or her people unconditionally. Leadership is a broad concept, and, for the purpose of this study, it is necessary to define leadership and identify the qualities of effective leaders as pertaining to K–12 education.

DEFINITION OF LEADERSHIP

Creighton (1999) and Kanji (2008) note that leadership is difficult to define. There is an absence of leadership models that illustrates how leadership works, and the concept is difficult to measure. Kanji states that much of the difficulty of measuring leadership stems from the constantly changing roles of leaders and the complex nature of a leadership position. Walker and Riordan (2010) claim that leadership is neither defined by the position nor limited to a single person. They believe that the role of the principal is important but that, when leadership is exercised by many and aligned with the goals of the school leader, it appears most successful.

Redick, Reyna, Schaffer, and Toomey (2014) believe that leaders must possess leadership competencies that are essential to lead successfully. Redick et al. devised the four-factor model of self-leadership, leading others, environment, and psychology. Gray (2000) claims that leadership requires a drive that must be used to influence people toward action and a unified vision.

To influence an entire organization, the leader must be willing to incite change within the group. The qualities of persistence and commitment provide an individual with the courage to lead and create change among the people of an organization (Stewart, 2004). Such change can occur only through intentional, sustained commitment by the leader of any organization. Finally, one must maintain the responsibilities of leadership at the forefront to be a successful leader (Weiss, 2007).

SCHOOL LEADERSHIP

Having well-prepared principals at the helm of schools is an investment in creating positive school environments for both the faculty and the student body. School leadership training programs should emphasize to future leaders the importance of developing a set of principles that will be communicated in schools daily and that are reflective of the needs of students and staff.

Peterson and Deal (1998) assert that school leaders are essential in the charge to foster a positive school culture. They define school culture as "the underground stream of norms, values, beliefs, traditions, and rituals that have built up over time." They believe that leaders responsible for a school must be cognizant of their school culture to understand their current situation and what they need to do to develop a successful school.

Walker and Riordan (2010) state that it is very important for school leaders to assess the educational and cultural norms that exist in their schools to find ways to develop collective capacity. Leaders must attempt to understand staff as people who are individuals and as members of collectives, regardless of where they come from or their different cultural backgrounds.

According to Peterson and Deal (1998), not only must the school leader be aware of the culture, but he or she also must monitor the culture continuously and work to make positive adjustments for a caring and nurturing school culture, which Stewart (2004) believes is the leader's most important task.

Starratt (2005) notes that leaders need to utilize care and compassion and must take responsibility for creating an environment in which the well-being of teachers and students is ensured. In addition, leaders' ability to take special care to nurture those affected by their decisions is essential—for example, a teacher whose assignment has been changed. The leader must attempt to understand the staff as individuals who are a part of a collective in which relationships are grounded in professionalism and humanity.

The leader must lead by example and inspire others to serve alongside him or her. Graseck (2005) states that leaders who dismiss the caring and nurturing dimension of leadership undermine the development of quality relationships and harm the school environment. School leaders equipped with the skill set to create nurturing school environments will motivate their school faculty to achieve a set of strategic initiatives. Weiss (2007) explains that it is critical to establish a positive working environment to achieve high standards.

Graseck (2005) believes that an effective school leader must make progress toward meeting local, state, and national standards. Graseck states that a school leader must assist the faculty in the effort of teaching children by modeling for the staff the desired behaviors and assisting the faculty when needed. When doing so, a school leader will bring his or her school closer to its goals.

Leaders must be inimitable individuals who are willing to take calculated risks to influence people within an organization to achieve their desired goals (Leithwood, Harris, & Hopkins, 2008). Bolman and Deal (2002) and Leithwood et al. (2008) believe that the impact of quality leaders occurs through the courage and optimism that they've manifested in their own developmental journey as well as their ability to look deep within themselves and to seek support and sustenance from colleagues to build their inner strength and confidence.

This strength and confidence enables them to bring their soul and spirit to their schools. Furthermore, such support provides the leader with strength and clarity to reflect upon the interpersonal and intrapersonal needs of the organization. These practices will equip a leader to become effective in dealing with the challenges and the stress that accompany the role (Walker & Riordan, 2010).

SCHOOL LEADERSHIP AND SPIRITUALITY

School leaders differentiate themselves from other leaders because they find motivation for their work that cannot be derived from money or recognition. Robertson (2008) presents the qualities of school leaders that enable them to lead successfully, improve society, and make real differences in young people's lives.

According to Robertson, a school leader must be sincere and able to look beyond the mundane managerial responsibilities of the job to personalize the nature of his or her work. This *head-and-heart* approach to leadership invokes a spiritual dimension. This connection between spiritual leadership and educational leadership is solidified as one begins to reorient his or her leadership as a deeply personal connection to oneself. Robertson argues that the traits emblematic of a spiritual leader, including compassion, integrity, and perseverance, are not exclusive to spiritual or religious professions but can be cultivated only when a spiritual or deeply personal connection is forged.

SPIRITUAL LEADERSHIP

Yusof and Tahir's (2011) work relates spiritual leadership theories to employee job satisfaction using a multidimensional approach. They note that the concept and definition of spirituality are well contested and that, although spirituality is often used interchangeably with religion, it is not the same as religion. They explain that whereas religion can be understood as belonging to a particular group or organization, spirituality is more intangible in nature and more encompassing than religion.

Fairholm (1997) explains spirituality as follows:

> Our spirituality is a source guide for personal values and meaning-making, a way of understanding the world, an inner awareness. It is a means of integration of the self and our world. Spirituality is another word for personal awareness. It is the acceptance of universal values that individuals believe guide their everyday actions and by which they judge their actions. Spirituality in organizations refers to the inner values of the leader and the followers—the mature principles, qualities, and influences that we implicitly exhibit in our behavior and interactions with other people.

Korac-Kakabadse, Kouzmin, and Kakabadse (2002) define a spiritual leader as an individual who places emphasis on values associated with spirituality as a guide in leading others. A spiritual leader builds shared values and meaning to foster growth in those who are being led. A central focus of spiritual leaders is on transforming toward a state of self-realization, which helps them to maintain a life purpose and allows them to lead effectively and nourish their own growth.

The concept of spirituality is more generally associated with leadership positions in faith-based professions. Nevertheless, Woods (2007) shows how spiritual experience has an impact on the practical, professional life of those who are in leadership positions in the schools. Woods surveyed head teachers in nondenominational and denominational state schools in three counties in England in regard to whether any spiritual experiences influenced their leadership.

Woods found that spiritual experiences are widespread among head teachers; spiritual experiences contribute greatly to teachers' personal capacities, such as their knowledge and emotional sensitivity; and the awareness caused by spiritual experiences contributes to their leadership and the meaning that they derive from their role as policy makers.

Woods states, "Good leadership draws on deep roots" and shows that productive leadership can derive its effectiveness from spiritual experience. Woods believes that the exploration of one's spiritual dimension allows an educational leader to cultivate a deeper appreciation and sense of purpose in his or her daily activities and that understanding the influence of spiritual experience on leadership in school communities provides a more comprehensive understanding of leadership in schools, in general, and advances the field, both theoretically and practically.

Keyes, Hanley-Maxwell, and Capper (1999) conducted an ethnographic study of a principal of an inclusive elementary school. They found that the principal's leadership behavior extended beyond a traditional empowering leadership model and was described by the faculty as "ethical, caring, humble, patient, and loving." Ethnographic accounts indicated that the principal believed that educational leadership went beyond religious affiliation to an association with personal dignity and individual value. Keyes et al.'s findings indicated:

> The empowering principal's behaviors in an inclusive school are undergirded by a spirituality grounded in six beliefs: the value of personal struggle, the dignity of all people, a merger of the personal and professional, confidence that people are doing their best, the importance of listening, and the importance of dreams.

Dantley (2003) believes that educational leaders who ground their work in purpose-driven leadership have a distinct advantage in facing daily professional challenges and are able to garner inner strength to mediate systemic inequities in the educational system. The concept of purposive leadership is an outgrowth of aggressive pessimism, a substitute for optimism, and a coping strategy in overcoming obstacles. Aggressive pessimism is often cited in describing the way that African Americans mediate numerous internal societal structures and systems that marginalize their identities and reinforce and reestablish the dominant power of elite groups.

According to Dantley, the application of purposive leadership by school leaders yields a change in their perspectives on academic goals and helps to guide their student population not only toward minimum competency but also toward a sense of purpose and commitment to societal change. Purpose-driven leaders are able to reorient their view on education and schools as not only solely spaces for academic pursuits but also for potential political and social change.

SPIRITUAL LEADERSHIP IN ISLAM

Shah (2006) studied the relationship between knowledge and leadership in Muslim societies from an Islamic perspective and in terms of how this relationship informs the concept of educational leadership. According to the classical Islamic scholar Tibawi, "the social, educational, and related notions and concepts in Muslim societies cannot be truly appreciated without some accurate understanding of the Islamic faith and civilization" (as cited in Shah, 2006). Shah notes how the Quran cites the teacher or leader (*Muallam*) as the highest authority in the Islamic social system. A teacher is vested with the same respect and responsibility as a parent and, consequently, has a great deal of accountability to his or her students.

Shah provides a three-dimensional model of educational leadership in Islam: (a) teaching with knowledge and understanding (educator), (b) guiding with wisdom and values (prophet/leader), and (c) caring with responsibility and commitment (parent). Based on this model, teaching, leading, and caring are equivalent. The fundamental aims of education are reinforced by faith, and moral values strengthen the role of teachers and make teaching both a professional and spiritual enterprise, in which "the teacher and a wider leadership role [are combined] into one."

LITERATURE ON SCHOOL LEADERSHIP

To date, there is no academic literature on American Muslim public school principals. To conduct this research study, the researcher had to draw on the experiences of Jewish and Catholic communities when they first arrived to the United States. Both communities certainly experienced hardship in their early days in the United States, in their neighborhoods, the schools they attended, their places of work, and in society as a whole (Takaki, 2008). Thus, research on these groups is useful to understanding the experience of Muslim Americans, who face prejudice and discrimination based on religious differences and international conflicts.

The prejudice and discrimination in regard to Jews and Catholics stem from religious bigotry that was perpetuated by the elitist attitudes of Protestants and by international conflicts, specifically, World War II. Catholics comprised Irish and Italians, and Jews were Eastern European immigrants who were perceived as racially and religiously different (Weiner, 2006).

THE JEWISH MIGRATION EXPERIENCE

The presence of Jews in the United States dates back to the founding of the New World in 1492 and perhaps even earlier. Hirschman and Yates (2012) report that, based on historical accounts, there were five Jews among the 90 sailors on Christopher Columbus's expedition. In 1654, 23 Jewish refugees migrated to the port of New Amsterdam, now known as New York City, and were the first Jews to establish a permanent Jewish community.

Upon settling in New Amsterdam, Jews faced discriminatory restrictions not faced by other immigrant groups. Peter Stuyvesant petitioned the Dutch West India Company to forbid Jews from settling in New Amsterdam. Nevertheless, the company approved entry with the stipulation that Jews would care for the Jews among them who were poor to avoid burdening the company or the community. This stipulation was known as the Stuyvesant promise, which was the impetus for self-help organizations created by Jews for Jews. These organizations provided Jews with the economic and educational support as well as defended the community from anti-Semitism (Wenger, 1996).

The first great migration from Russia and Poland to the United States began in the 1870s and lasted through the 1920s. Many European Jews considered the United States to be the Promised Land. Religious freedom, the opportunity to secure a free education for their children, and the chance to achieve the American dream lured them to the United States. Many Jews made New York City their destination, and it became home to the largest concentration of Jews globally. The majority of Jews in New York City lived in the Lower East Side of Manhattan, Harlem, Brownsville, and Flatbush Brooklyn. Jews lived tightly together, segregated from other communities.

RELIGIOUS PREJUDICE EXPERIENCED BY JEWS

The United States was not as welcoming or freely accommodating as the Eastern European Jews had thought. Jews faced anti-Semitism and institutional discrimination in business, higher education, and government legislation, which affected their livelihood. In 1924, the U.S. government passed the National Origins Act to limit the number of people who entered the United States. The act was designed to favor people of Anglo-Saxon origin and disenfranchise Jews and other minorities, such as Japanese, Chinese, and people from the Asian Pacific Triangle.

This was evident during the time of the Great Depression and in the 1930s and 1940s, when Jews were seeking refuge from Nazi persecution during World War II but were denied entry. Based on a U.S. public opinion poll, there was considerable anti-Semitism, with 67–83% of individuals opposing the migration of Jewish refugees. Due to public opinion and the immigration quota, the United States would not make an exception to permit the entry of 10,000 Jewish refugee children (Berger, 2010).

Anti-Semitic propaganda in the 1930s was heard on the airwaves and on the House floor in a congressional hearing, at which Congressman L. T. McFadden stated that Jews, as communist infiltrators, were conspiring to bring down the U.S. government and its economy. McFadden made his claim by referencing the libel publication *The Protocols of the Elders of Zion*.

Anti-Semitism was most effectively spread on radio talk shows, notably by Father Charles E. Coughlin, who became a threat to Jewish groups. Father Coughlin's radio show had a listenership of more than 14 million Americans and even had a large audience in New York. When the radio station WMCA took Father Coughlin's show off the air, 5,000 people picketed the station and demanded Father Coughlin's return. This anti-Semitism was also expressed in physical violence against Jews. The worst attacks were in Boston, where Father Coughlin had a large following. According to an official investigation, on average, there were two attacks a month and perhaps more, but these were unreported.

THE VALUE OF EDUCATION FOR JEWS

As for Christians and Muslims, education is a central tenet of the Jewish faith. Education was essential for learning to read and for studying the Torah. It is believed that Jewish education begins at the age of infancy. When parents teach their children the Hebrew alphabet, they are not just teaching them how to read but also teaching them to pray. Jewish children are taught to revere and respect their ancient heritage and the scholars who have studied the divine teachings for generations (Lubinsky, 1980). "The priorities were such that food and education were interchangeable, with clothing and shelter trailing distantly behind."

Jewish parents who migrated to the United States from the 1870s to the 1920s had, for the first time in their history, the opportunity to have their children educated in the public school system, free of charge, with no restrictions. Jews enrolled their children, who had little or no English language knowledge, in New York City public schools, where they were teased and taunted about their culture and customs.

In 1910, the Lower East Side of Manhattan accounted for 46% of the total elementary school enrollment. Then, in 1914, New York City public schools had another influx of immigrants, with an enrollment of approximately 808,000 students. Of those students 277,000 were Jews. While Jewish children attended public schools, their parents ensured that their children maintained a strong Jewish identity through receiving instruction in Hebrew and Jewish history and culture at local synagogues and supported the rabbinical tradition of Torah study in the United States.

Torah study is an honorable profession within the Jewish community and, historically, has been practiced by men. Men who choose this path make the commitment to pass down Jewish law and knowledge to future generations, and their wives work to support the family. Jewish women's role in education was to have a basic education so that they could teach young girls elementary skills in reading and writing Yiddish.

Women were not permitted to teach in any official capacity. The notion of women being charged with educating both boys and girls was unheard of among most Central and Eastern European Jews. Teaching and learning had been traditionally reserved for male-dominated religious tradition (Weiner, 2006).

Many Jews also flocked to institutions of higher learning. In the 1920s, Hunter College and New York City College were about 80% Jewish (Sachar, 1992). Jews also attended Ivy League schools, such as Harvard University, where Jewish enrollment was about 22%, and Yale University, where Jewish enrollment was 18%. Such enrollment did not last long, however, after the rise of anti-Semitism, at which point the number of students began to decline due to discriminatory practices. Jewish enrollment at Harvard dropped to 10% by 1928 and to 8% at Yale by the 1930s.

ROLE OF JEWS IN PUBLIC EDUCATION AND THE PRINCIPALSHIP

As noted, teaching and learning have been reserved for males in the Jewish tradition. This began to change in the United States, however, when Jewish women flocked to the world of education, both public and Jewish. For the past 150 years, Jewish women have played a critical role in the public school system. Dating back to the 19th century, the teaching profession became feminized by a group of middle-class women who sought a prestigious place in society.

Many Jewish women gravitated to teaching for the level of respect and prestige that the field offered women who dedicated their lives to serving instead of marriage. Among these Jewish women was Julia Richman, the daughter of German-speaking immigrants from Prague, Bohemia. Richman was very influential in her community and in the field of education. In 1884, she became the first Jew to be named a grammar public school principal. Richman was determined to establish cohesive programs, with other educators that addressed students' social, emotional, and academic needs. By 1903, Richman was elevated to district superintendent of the Lower East Side schools.

The number of Jewish teachers and principals continued to increase in New York City as more Jews migrated to the United States. New York City public schools began to offer Hebrew as a class, certified by the Board of Regents, from 1908 until 1923, but the decreasing enrollment of students due to the curtailment of immigration resulted in its discontinuation.

A reemergence of the Hebrew program debuted in 1930 in predominantly Jewish neighborhoods with Jewish principals. Among the public school principals who addressed the Hebrew language need were Dr. Elias Lieberman and Dr. Gabriel Mason of Lincoln and Jefferson High Schools, respectively.

Research on American Jews in the field of education has focused on students, teachers, the curriculum, the settings, and the community and, more recently, on the retention of administrators in Jewish day schools. There is, however, a lack of research on Jewish principals' lived experiences in Jewish day schools and, for that matter, the public school system. This exclusion of the Jewish principals in the literature also is referenced in Kelman's (1992) review of research on Jewish education, which illustrates that there is not a single study on the educational leadership of Jewish principals.

Yacobi (1998) also notes the scarcity of research on Jewish American principals by drawing attention to the initiatives and research on Jewish education, dating as far back as the late 1990s. Yacobi states, "Although the leadership role of the educator is mentioned in passing in the literature, there has been little call for specialized preparation, knowledge or recognition of the professional role."

One study (Gottlieb, 2007), conducted by a student in a master's program at the University of Toronto, focused on the student's experience in a Jewish supplementary school. Gottlieb states that the supplementary school environment is filled with academic and institutional challenges among staff, families, and school board and can result in a "wounding" of the leadership lives of Jewish educators, the primary cause of which is a community culture that neither encourages nor supports the expression of the educator's practice and/or personal values and beliefs.

Gottlieb hopes that his research will provide a means for Jewish educators to reflect on their own practice, spark debate on the difficulties of being a Jewish educator, and provide new ideas on the role of a Jewish educator.

MIGRATION AND SETTLEMENT OF CATHOLICS IN THE UNITED STATES

Members of the Catholic religion, like those of Islam, comprise many ethnic and racial groups. The ethnic groups that played a critical role in Catholicism over the course of U.S. history include Spanish, Irish, English, French, Italian, and German (Takaki, 2008). The first form of migration of Catholics was motivated by the desire to flee religious persecution and to find economic opportunities.

The migration of Catholics to the New World began in 1565. In that year, the Spanish brought Catholicism to the North American continent when they set sail from Spain to the New World, settling in St. Augustine, Florida. By 1634, Catholicism had made its way to the British North American colonies, where three English Jesuit priests had settled in Maryland and established the first Jesuit mission under the English Province of the Society of Jesus.

The second form of migration occurred through the slave trade, through which Irish war captives were involuntarily brought and sold as indentured servants in Virginia in the early 17th century. Catholicism then continued to expand over the 17th and 18th centuries. By the 1830s, the number of Catholics surged as new immigrants settled in northern and urban areas. According to O'Gorman (1985), there was a 40% increase in Catholics in the United States between 1830 and 1880, composed of Catholics of Irish and German backgrounds.

Based on their living in a society that was predominantly Protestant, life for Catholics was filled with hardship. Although the two faiths shared similar theology and spirituality, Catholics were singled out for their sacramental practices. Historically, Catholics and Protestants have been in conflict, which Protestants felt would end only with the defeat of the antichrist, whom the Protestants believed was the pope, as Protestants feared the formation of a monarchy by Catholic papists.

According to Burgess (2012), "Early modern Protestants on both sides of the Atlantic believed that they were engaged in a world-wide struggle against the pope, as Antichrist, and his foot soldiers." This is rooted in a theological belief shared by early Reformation Protestant thinkers, and Protestants used every means to spread their anti-Catholic propaganda.

Regardless of anti-Catholic ideology, the Maryland Jesuit missionaries were driven to achieve three goals: converting Native Americans, reconciling Protestants to the Catholic Church, and administering sacraments to the believers. These goals were met with distrust and mistreatment. The Protestants feared a takeover by the Catholic Church and viewed themselves as targets of the Catholic menace. This fear grew stronger upon the Protestants' learning of a Catholic colony in Canada that infiltrated Native American lands and converted indigenous inhabitants to Catholicism, a population who later became soldiers in New France (Stanwood, 2005).

Intellectual Protestants viewed Catholicism as a superstitious religion with the primary objective to convert and control ignorant populations. During the 16th and 17th centuries, the rise of printing provided an outlet to spread the dangers of Catholic missionaries and their agenda of popery and violent methods, which Catholics used to achieve their "diabolical" program. "Popular literature often described the Catholic threat in terms of gender and sexuality, portraying papists as sexual predators who targeted Protestant women and children for special treatment" (Stanwood, 2005). The fear of Catholics reached to the Puritan colonies in New England and farther south to the majority Dutch colony of New York.

From 1700 to 1850, Catholics experienced an onslaught of attacks on their beliefs; however, the number of Catholics continued to grow, along with the migration of additional Irish and German Europeans. In the midst of this growth, anti-Catholicism pervaded the colonies through the distribution of *The New England Primer*.

Literary attacks were made by notables, such as Samuel B. F. Morris, who wrote the *Foreign Conspiracy* on the papal plot; Maria Monk, who wrote *Awful Disclosures*, which offered malicious depictions of Catholic priests and nuns; and political cartoonist Thomas Nast, who drew links between Catholic hierarchy and tyranny. Catholics were deprived of most of their civil and political rights in English colonies, with the exception of Pennsylvania.

By the 1840s, the outgrowth of anti-Catholicism resulted in nativist civil riots against Catholics, forcing the closure of Catholic churches in Philadelphia, the burning of convents in Boston, and the taking of arms by Catholics to defend themselves on the streets of New York. By the 1850s, anti-Catholicism evolved into political and economic discrimination. The marginalization of Catholics by Protestants made its way into children's literature, in which Catholics were portrayed as cultural and religious outsiders. As noted by Malcolm (2011):

> The American Protestant children were inculcated to believe the very worst of the Catholic priest—not only that he was a conniving and evil person, but also

that his ability to know everything that went on in his parish bordered on the otherworldly.

THE VALUE OF EDUCATION FOR CATHOLICS

Catholics believe that the teaching mission of the Church comes directly from Christ himself. As followers of the faith, they must fulfill this mandate to all Catholics through Church bishops. According to Davis (2004), "The bishops believed that survival depended on morality, and religion played a major role in mankind's continued existence, and home, church, and schools were the three institutions which played a part in developing mankind."

O'Gorman (1985) notes that ministry and religious education must be identified with the Church's mandate as follows: (a) forming community, (b) ministering the word, (c) serving the people, (d) ministering God's judgment, and (e) ministering the sacraments, and education is the sole outlet to deliver these mandates, as they were delivered by Jesus Himself.

These mandates continue to be paramount and the focal point of the Catholic Church. The U.S. Conference of Catholic Bishops (2015) currently promotes these mandates on its website. It begins by referencing the following verse from the Bible, in which Jesus says to his apostles, "Go therefore and make disciples of all nations, baptizing them in the name of the Father and of the Son and of the Holy Spirit, teaching them to observe all that I have commanded you" (Matthew 28:19–20, English Standard Version).

The U.S. Conference of Catholic Bishops proclaimed that it is the duty of Catholics to spread the *Word of God* widely, as transmitted by Christ's apostles. In doing so, they are involved in the lifelong effort of forming people into witnesses to Christ and opening their hearts to be spiritually transformed, as prescribed by the Holy Spirit.

Catholics were determined to deliver this education to their children and community, as a whole, by all means possible, at a time where these teachings were not recognized and looked down upon by the mainstream U.S. communities in which they lived. In this regard, O'Gorman (1985) states:

> The story of the means of Catholic education moves from upper class, to lower class, to middle class concerns. During the 1830 to 1875 period, the Catholic Church in the U.S. subsequently followed three plans for the education of its people. The first plan established colleges and seminaries fashioned after the schools that the other churches in this country conducted at the time of the revolution. This was Catholic aristocratic education. The second plan, that fostered by John Hughes, was modeled after the benevolent schools run by charitable institutions funded by the state. By the close of this period, Bernard McQuaid had already begun the third plan that would become the paradigm for the twentieth century—parochial schools for all (the middle class schools).

CATHOLIC EDUCATION

Catholics, like Jews and African Americans, were perceived by a largely Protestant school system as racially and religiously different social outcasts. Catholics, as well, faced a great deal of discrimination and were subjected to citizenship training to become civilized, White, productive American citizens. Public schools did not provide Catholic children with a meaningful education, as was offered to Protestant children.

Due to their immigrant status, Catholic children were given instruction in manual arts and home economics classes, which provided them with the means to be a low-skilled laborer. As a result, Catholic (and Jewish) families pulled their children out of the public school system at the age of 14 to work in factories.

The inefficient schooling of Catholic children and misconceptions and perceptions created about Catholics by Protestants in the mid-19th century led Catholics to seek public money to open their own schools in the United States. Protestants saw the creation of separate Catholic schools as a ploy to destroy their existing education system, to spread inaccurate information about history, and to deprive Catholic children's exposure to God's scripture. Protestants believed that these schools undermined the assimilation required to make Catholics proper American citizens.

By 1829, the First Provincial Council of Baltimore, a body comprising the hierarchy of the Catholic Church in the United States and the Third Plenary Council, decreed the necessity to establish additional Catholic schools in places where there were no parish schools to meet the needs of Catholic families. After this declaration was made, additional Catholic schools slowly but steadily became a reality. Davis (2004) notes:

> In 1887, the year these decrees were to go into effect, there were 6,910 churches and 2,697 of them had a school. In 1913 there 9,500 Catholic parishes in this country and 5,250 had schools. Finally, by 1933 there were 12,537 Catholic Churches in the United States, and there were 7,462 Catholic schools.

By the early 1900s, Catholic parochial schools gained legal legitimacy through two U.S. Supreme Court decisions.

Things began to change for Catholic Americans following World War II, based on historically significant events, including the passage of the GI Bill, which created higher economic standard opportunities for many Catholics, as well as the election of John F. Kennedy, the first Catholic to serve as president of the United States.

By 1965, after the Second Vatican Council meeting in Rome, Catholic education experienced a huge transformation. The Vatican Council watered down the Catholic education principles created by the Third Plenary Council.

Youniss and Convey (2000) report that these cataclysmic changes were the Catholic Church's approach to encourage a greater connection to the secular world and an abandonment of its traditional teachings, but these alterations caused many Catholics to reassess their religious values and practices.

The ripple effect of these changes was evident in the drop in student enrollment, which resulted in the loss of Catholic clergy between 1965 and 2002. Thousands of priests and nuns became disenchanted with their religious commitment to the Church, ultimately leading them to return to laity.

This exodus of priests and nuns created a teacher deficit, which needed to be filled. Catholic schools were forced to hire thousands of lay teachers who, as compared to clergy teachers who had dedicated their lives to the Church, did not come at low salaries. Lay teachers, who had families, needed a higher salary and benefits. Unfortunately, these requirements increased Catholic school tuition costs.

PUBLIC EDUCATION

The role or lived experiences of Catholic teachers or principals in public education has not been widely studied. Upon searching the literature, the researcher found three studies on the role or experiences of teachers and principals, which are discussed below. The studies did not specifically seek teachers or principals of Catholic backgrounds, yet the teachers and principal in these studies self-identified as Catholic or as being raised as Catholic but not practicing.

The anti-Catholic sentiment made it difficult for Catholic children and teachers to fit into public schools; however, they persevered. In this regard, Collins (2006) provides a history of Catholic teachers in the New York City public schools. She studied the role of race, ethnicity, and gender in the evolution of a feminized profession as well as examined the various institutions that shaped the demographics of the New York City public school teaching force over the 20th century.

Collins focused on why the city had the lowest proportion of minority teachers to minority students. She used archival sources and a variety of materials to analyze the institutions that were primarily responsible for teacher education, recruitment, licensing, hiring, and promotion in the school system. Collins found that racially discriminatory practices and institutional racism were largely at play for the low numbers of minority teachers in the profession.

Collins also noted that Catholic teachers who served in the public schools were admitted to the City University of New York (CUNY) teacher education program at a higher rate than were their Jewish counterparts. By 1950, however, that changed, and Jewish teachers at that time comprised 65% of the teaching force. At the same time, Catholic teachers were threatened by the demographic changes in the school system and the religious accommodations being requested by Jewish teachers. As a result, in 1948, the Brooklyn chapter of the Catholic Teachers Association took issue with a proposal presented by an interfaith teachers' organization that sought to grant Jewish teachers three Jewish holy days as citywide holidays.

As years progressed, the number of teachers who were Catholic increased after the city and state eliminated government funding for religious schools. This forced district officials to recruit more Catholic teachers while the city was taking over some of these schools. Collins also noted that Irish Catholic teachers gained access to teaching positions through their ethnic connections with politically influential leaders.

As the number of Catholic teachers increased, they, too, formed an association similar to the kind formed by Protestant and Jewish teachers. By the 1930s, Irish Catholics managed the Board of Education headquarters (also known as 110 Livingston Street), which kept down the promotion of Jewish teachers for principal positions and maintained the hostilities between Catholics and Jews.

CATHOLIC PRINCIPALS

Dalia (2005) examined the relationship between school leadership and spirituality by conducting interviews with 10 principals from both public and Catholic schools in Ontario. Study participants were Christian and White, and, of the 10 participants, three self-identified as practicing Catholics and one self-identified as a former Catholic.

Dalia's findings indicated that spirituality played an important role in shaping the principals' leadership practices. The principals felt that their spirituality was closely connected to their personal core values and, therefore, fortified their work as principals. The public school principals also indicated that they felt uncomfortable expressing religious beliefs or spirituality in Ontario public schools. Dalia recommended that future researchers should examine spirituality across different cultures to provide a more representative and inclusive theory of spirituality and school leadership.

Robertson (2008) examined spirituality as it relates to the overall job satisfaction and resiliency of principals in public schools. The study participants included 80 principals, from two rural and three urban school districts, of which the majority were from the Bible Belt. Among these 80 participants, five identified as Catholic. Robertson asked all principals to complete a number of assessments of spiritual leadership, job satisfaction, and resilience.

Robertson found a statistically significant relationship between spirituality and resilience but not between spirituality and job satisfaction. Based on this finding, Robertson used multiple regression to analyze the relationship between resilience and the principals' demographics and found a statistically significant relationship between resilience and gender, and resilience and religious affiliation. Robertson recommended that future researchers examine the relationship between a leader's spirituality and academic achievement in schools and the relationship between a leader's spirituality and school climate.

It is intended for the researcher to use the Jewish and Catholic experience in the United States as a way of contextualizing the experience of Muslims in America. While the Muslim American experience may differ in many ways, there are certainly similarities given the minority status along with forms of discrimination that they are faced with. It is hoped that through this book, more research can be conducted on Muslim public school leaders in the future.

KEY CHAPTER IDEAS

- Scholars offer a variety of definitions for leadership and school leadership.
- It is understood that spiritual leadership and educational leadership can both be concepts simultaneously that school leaders seek to embrace in their role, as both can emphasize the importance of certain values.
- In the Islamic tradition, the aims of education are reinforced by faith, and moral values strengthen the role of teachers and make teaching a professional and spiritual experience.
- Presently, there is no academic literature on Muslim public school leaders; thus the researcher chooses to present work on the Catholic and Jewish experience in America, for the purpose of understanding the context of religious minorities and education in the United States.

Chapter Three

The American Muslim Experience

The Lost-Found Nation of Islam in the Wilderness of North America.

The experience of Muslims in America certainly has its own set of unique aspects, yet there are also points of similarities between Muslims and other minority groups in this nation. Namely, the struggles of building a strong sense of identity, seeking a proper education, and having fair representation in all realms of professional life.

As this study is specifically focused on the experience of school leaders, it is important to note that studies relay there is a shortage of qualified school leaders. It is attributed to the high standards of accountability under the No Child Left Behind Act (NCLB), the high stress of the job, and low salaries. This shortage is a national crisis that school districts and university school leadership programs have shown some progress in, but proportionate increases in minority principals remain stagnant.

In 2003–2004, 82.4% of the public school principals in the United States were White, while only 17.6% were minority principals. Nationally, 10.6% were Black and 5.3% were Hispanic. Sanchez, Thornton, and Usinger (2009) conclude "that there are not enough principals of color, and the enrollment of prospective, minority principal candidates in educational preparation programs must become a high priority." While the number of African American school leaders is 10.6% nationally, there has been a focus on learning more about their experiences in the private and public school sector.

There have been a number of studies that have been done on African American school leaders. The body of work that exists on African American school leaders focuses exclusively on urban African American school leaders, both female and male. Gooden (2012) claims that much of the literature that exists about African American school leaders in the last century was done by researchers outside of the African American community and, according to Gooden, does not capture the authentic experiences or perspectives of African Americans.

Such studies essentially have encouraged research on other school leaders of different minorities in the realm of education, to achieve authenticity and a deeper understanding of the American minority experience as a whole. Such studies can potentially draw deeper similarities between the minority experience of African American, Muslim, Hispanic, and Asian backgrounds.

ARRIVAL OF AFRICAN AMERICAN MUSLIMS THROUGH THE SLAVE TRADE

The presence of Muslims in the United States dates back to the early 1500s. In the year 1528, a slave named Estevanico from Morocco was shipwrecked with Spanish explorers in what is known today as Texas (Manseau, 2015). Following that, the first great wave of Muslims entering America began from the time of the slave trade. It is estimated that 12 million Africans were brought to North America as slaves, and that 20% of that population were Muslim.

It is important to note that the migration of African Americans to the United States was very different from Catholics, Jews, Muslims, and other ethnic groups that migrated to the United States. The migration of Africans into the Americas was not one of choice, but of force through the slave trade (Schiller, 2011). The presence of African Americans in the United States dates back to 1619, when the first 20 Africans were shipped on Dutch ships to Jamestown, Virginia, where they were destined for slavery. The sale of slaves was lucrative among the Dutch, Spanish, and Portuguese who captured and sold slaves in North and South America in the late 16th and early 17th centuries.

Africans were imported as slaves to New York State, Boston, Massachusetts Bay, and Plymouth, which were the first colonies to legitimize slavery through legislation under the 1641 Body of Liberties. These were then followed by Connecticut in 1650, Virginia in 1661, Maryland in 1663, New York and New Jersey in 1664, South Carolina in 1682, Rhode Island and Pennsylvania in 1700, North Carolina in 1715, and Georgia in 1750.

In 1645, the triangular slave trade launched with a ship from Boston that took slaves to the West Indies to trade them for sugar, tobacco, and liquor. During this period, Newport, Rhode Island, and Salem, Massachusetts, became major ports, which began the extensive introduction of African slaves into the British West Indies where they were sold to work on the sugar plantations. Over the course of 50 years, Charles Town (Charleston), South Carolina, became the largest mainland slave market. By 1790, the North

American slave trade grew significantly by 700,000 slaves, and by 1830 there were 2 million.

After arriving in America, many of the Muslim slaves were forced to abandon their faith although there were a number who practiced in secret. There are records of several slaves throughout the years; one notable former slave, Peter Salem, whose last name was originally Saleem, was a Muslim who fought in the Battle of Bunker Hill in 1775 and the American Revolution.

THE BIRTH OF THE NATION OF ISLAM

One of the first African Americans to publicly proclaim Islam as his religion was Timothy Drew, born in 1886 in North Carolina (Sahib, 1995). He found Islam to be a vehicle for Americans of African heritage to reconnect with their ancestors, and through his preaching, Drew developed a following. He changed his name to Noble Drew Ali and established the Moorish Science Temple of America in Newark, New Jersey, in 1913. In 1929, shortly after Drew Ali's death, a group that called itself "The Lost-Found Nation of Islam in the Wilderness of North America" arose in Detroit and was led by a man believed to be of Turkish or Iranian origin, W. D. Fard. Fard appealed to African Americans who desired spiritual uplifting and developed a following.

Fard received invitations from many community members who were interested in discussing Islam. The demand for more discussion led Fard to establish the first University of Islam in 1932. In the beginning stage of his preaching, he was recognized as a messenger and later as some sort of deity figure. As Fard continued to preach, approximately 8,000 Blacks in Detroit became members of the Nation of Islam (NOI). One of his followers was Elijah Muhammad, who became a companion to Fard and later became the supreme minister of the NOI in 1934 after Fard mysteriously disappeared.

Elijah Muhammad led a large portion of the Black community in Detroit and Chicago. His objective was to reach the masses of underprivileged Blacks who were oppressed by the "White man." Under his leadership, ministers were recruited to spread the message of the NOI. One of the most prominent ministers was Malcolm X, and the 1950s and 1960s were the most significant time for the NOI in terms of growth. However this growth did not last, as tensions between Elijah Muhammad and Malcolm X developed that led Muhammad to suspend Malcolm X for a speech that he made after the assassination of President Kennedy.

Elijah Mohammad continued to lead the NOI as his son was coming of age. In 1975, he died, and his son Wallace (Warith) Deen Muhammad assumed spiritual leadership. According to Haddad (1998):

Warith Deen Muhammad recognized the importance of bringing the Nation of Islam into the mainstream of Islam and immediately began the difficult process of closing the gaps between his father's doctrines and orthodox Islam, the Quranic teachings (of a) world Muslim community, rather than as a strictly black nationalist movement.

This transition was influenced by Warith's personal study of Arabic, the Quran, and Islamic law and an exchange of ideas with Malcolm X after he himself underwent a religious transformation in Mecca. The NOI under Warith went through some name changes to distinguish itself from his father's teachings and as a means to become more mainstream within the broader Muslim community in the United States. In 1985, the movement began to transition into identifying themselves as Sunni Muslims (Haddad, 1998).

MIGRATION AND SETTLEMENT OF IMMIGRANT MUSLIMS IN THE UNITED STATES

Following the initial presence of Black Muslims in America, it was then immigrant communities that arrived to the country and established Muslim institutions to meet their needs. A large number of these Muslim immigrants entered the United States between World Wars I and II from parts of the Ottoman Empire, including today's Syria, Lebanon, Jordan, Turkey, Yugoslavia, and Albania, as well as people from the Indo-Pakistani continent.

In 1907, Tatar immigrants from Poland, Russia, and Lithuania formed the American Mohammedan Society, the nation's first Muslim organization. In 1934, the Mother Mosque of America, built in Cedar Rapids, Iowa, became the first mosque in the United States. To meet the educational needs of these Muslim groups, the first Muslim Students Association (MSA) was formed in 1963 at the University of Illinois with the agenda of discussing issues that affected Muslims. Over the years, MSA chapters were formed at universities across the United States.

The next wave of Muslim immigration began after the Immigration and Nationality Act of 1965 allowed entry of people from Asia, Africa, and the Middle East. The existing MSAs were not able to address the needs of new immigrants and thus, the Islamic Society of North America (ISNA) was formed. The needs of the Muslim community continued to grow in the 1970s and 1980s, leading to the development of additional organizations, such as the Islamic Circle of North America (ICNA), the American Society of Muslims (ASM), and the Muslim American Society (MAS).

The formation of organizations such as the Muslim Public Affairs Council (MPAC) in 1989 and the Council on American–Islamic Relations (CAIR) in 1995 was and continues to be instrumental in bringing Muslim concerns into the political arena (Moore, 2007). Despite broader inclusivity, Muslim

American political action and legal mobilization remained in their formative stages during the 1990s. According to Leonard (2005), these emergent Muslim leadership organizations are a consequence of the growing tensions between American Muslims and U.S. political leaders and agendas.

The rise and importance of national American Muslim groups such as MPAC and CAIR coincide with the increase in civil rights and civil liberties violations, such as involuntary government interviews, detainment, deportation, racial profiling, surveillance, and suspicion of Muslims under the legislative measures of the USA PATRIOT Act.

DEMOGRAPHICS OF MUSLIMS IN THE UNITED STATES TODAY

Islam is considered to be the fastest growing religion in the world. A number of studies conducted in 2012 estimated the number of Muslims at 3,480,000 in North America, while others indicate there are approximately about 8 million in the United States. It is also indicated that this number continues to grow due to immigration and high birthrates within Muslim communities. It is also important to note that while observing the demographic trend, the Muslim community also continues to increase its participation in politics and economic affairs, along with making contributions to the fields of science, engineering, business, and medicine.

In survey research, Younis (2009) found Muslim American women in the United States are one of the most highly educated groups, following Jewish American women. Younis also found that Muslim Americans have varying political views: 39% of young Muslim Americans consider their views moderate, 28% state they are either liberal or very liberal, and 20% see themselves as politically conservative or very conservative. When Muslims were asked whether religion was an important part of their daily lives, 80% answered in the affirmative, followed by 76% of Protestants, 68% of Catholics, and 39% of Jews. However, of the religious groups studied, 85% of Mormons answered in the affirmative.

As with other religions, adherents to Islam come from a variety of faith traditions and denominations. Sunni Muslims are widely recognized as the largest sect in Islam, comprising approximately 87–90% of Muslims worldwide. The second largest group identifies as Shia. Sunnis, Shias, and other Muslim-faith traditions share certain core beliefs, and each community has practices and beliefs that may be unique. Like other religions, the larger denominations are sometimes subdivided by different schools of thought. Accordingly, in addition to the broad cultural, racial, and ethnic diversity within Islam, there is also a diversity of theology and practice.

According to Moore (2007), Muslim Americans have earned salaries that afford them high standards of living. He also notes that a study conducted by

Columbia University School of Social Work shows that, in the aftermath of 9/11, the earnings of Arab and Muslim men have dropped by 10%. Despite this fluctuation, the pursuit of education in the Muslim American community is above the national average, with over 50% of Muslim Americans earning college and postgraduate degrees.

Moore attributes the economic and educational success of Muslims in America to the anonymity of Muslim communities during the 1970s and 1980s. Muslims leveraged this anonymity to concentrate on economic advancement rather than integration and civic engagement. In the aftermath of 9/11, as American Muslims faced religious prejudice and discrimination, they realized that they could no longer live as they did before.

THE EFFECTS OF 9/11

The attacks on the World Trade Center on September 11, 2001, was one of the most documented events in history. The attack and its aftermath became a media spectacle as the images and discourse used in the coverage of the attacks framed the terrorist attacks in a particular way that generated war hysteria, as suggested by Kellner (2003). He claims that the failure to responsibly report the event by the mainstream media created a platform through which dualisms between Islamic terrorism and civilization or good and evil were generated.

Kellner argues that the propagation of this sort of "clash of civilization" narrative was engineered to garner support for military retaliation. There are several studies that suggest that the 9/11 attacks exacerbated the problem of Islamophobia and ultimately made anti-Muslim rhetoric more acceptable. It is suggested that media spectacle was employed both by terrorists and the Bush administration to further their own respective agendas surrounding the 9/11 attacks. This fear tactic was a means to further the Bush administration's political agendas, which included a military upgrade.

The terrorist attacks on September 11 targeted specific symbols that represented the West and global capitalism. Kellner refers to the attack on the World Trade Center as a "terror spectacle," which was met with a response of halting or shutting down activity in major cities throughout the United States. As a means to deconstruct and demystify media spectacle, Kellner advocates a critical cultural studies approach to the discourses, images, and policies that may circulate in our media-saturated environment.

Although Islamophobia existed before 9/11, the attacks gave Islamophobia greater societal weight and consequently allowed Islamophobic expressions to have more societal acceptability as witnessed today in 2018. Just a few days before the 9/11 attacks, the United Nations formally recognized Islamophobia as anti-Muslim and anti-Islamic prejudice, discrimination, and hatred. The fact that the United Nations recognized the issue of Islamophobia confirms that anti-Muslim sentiment was a growing global concern.

Undoubtedly, the terrorist attacks have heightened tensions and the dissemination of fear toward Muslims in public sphere and media depiction. Ultimately, the portrayal of Muslims has been normalized to the extent that it has become common sense, truth, and reality. Nacos and Torres-Reyna (2002) tracked the shifts and changes in how the U.S. news media represented Muslim Americans over an 18-month period, including after the terrorist attacks on September 11. They studied four daily newspapers' coverage of American Muslims and Arab Americans and found that, in the post-9/11 period, Muslims and Arab Americans were referred to far more frequently.

The study noted that the most important change occurred with respect to the topics concerning Muslims and how they were reported. There was stereotypical coverage of Muslims pre-9/11, but the framing of news dramatically shifted toward more of an emphasis on Muslim and Arab American civil rights issues.

Ibrahim (2010) also studied the framing of Islam in the news and found that the visual frames and discourse used in the coverage of Islam in America post-9/11 were subjective and emphasized only certain aspects of Islam that were in agreement with certain ideologies. Ibrahim noted that media framing is inherently a subjective process whereby certain problems are heightened, and other realities are left out, and found that the discourse surrounding the terms *Arab* and *Islam* occurred in the context of violence. Ibrahim explains that it was only after the White House announced that the religion was one of peace, in response to an increase in hate crimes against Muslims, did the framing of Islam in the media begin to shift accordingly.

As a consequence of the 9/11 attacks, there is an ever-expanding political discourse of fear and terrorism in the United States. The relentless level of Islamophobic discourse during the 2008 Obama presidential campaign, and more prevalently the 2016 Trump presidential campaign, are indicators of this penetration of fear. The normalization of Islamophobic discourse in the 2008 election marks what some call the "third phase of Islamophobia" or the "institutionalized version of Islamophobia," which increased dramatically after 9/11 (Ali, 2012).

For example, the transformation of the word *Muslim* into a slur by Obama's opponents, by alleging he was a "closet Muslim" during the 2008 election, presented American Muslims as antithetical or threatening to American values. In the case of Republican candidate John McCain, his vice-presidential running mate Sarah Palin claimed that because of his suggested affiliations, "Obama's pallin' around with terrorists."

At a campaign event, McCain had posed the question to his supporters, "Who is the real Barack Obama?" to which the audience responded, a "terrorist!" The attack on Obama, namely, and his alleged affiliation with Bill

Ayers continued on the McCain/Palin campaign trail. At another event, a McCain supporter publicly expressed her distrust of Obama by saying, "He's an Arab!" The "mob fear" that the Republican campaign initiated on Obama's person led to a base of Republican constituents to believe that Obama was an Arab, a Muslim, and a terrorist.

The continued speculation of Obama's affiliation with the religion of Islam played a significant role in the campaign, as his "secret Muslim status" was increasingly seen as an acceptable attack and consequently an implementation of Islamophobia during the 2008 election. This was because the suggestion of Obama's status as a Muslim was overwhelmingly met with a denial that he was not a Muslim, as opposed to challenging this rhetoric with a clear condemnation of the prejudice that the accusation implied.

Such an attack eventually became a point of importance for the 2016 presidential candidate Donald Trump. During Obama's presidency, Trump had challenged Obama to provide official documentation of his birth in the United States, as he continuously accused Obama of being born in Kenya and a secret Muslim.

The Trump campaign of 2016 witnessed a much more significant level of Islamophobia. Throughout his early campaigning, Trump presented rhetoric such as "Islam hates us" and had proposed "a complete and total ban of Muslims," which after his election victory became an official executive order. The individuals he brought forth on his campaign trail and later administration would also make statements that claimed Islam is a "cancer" and overall claiming that Islam and Muslims present an imminent danger to American ideology.

One clear note of difference from previous administrations is that there was little distinction even between the notion of radicalized Muslims versus mainstream Muslims. The rhetoric even extended to suggest that Islam is not a religion, but simply a political ideology that requires some sort of militant action. This rhetoric has had a clear impact on the rise of hate crimes and bullying against American Muslims.

RELIGIOUS PREJUDICE EXPERIENCED BY AMERICAN MUSLIMS

The religious prejudice and discrimination of American Muslims date back to the time of slavery. To justify their enslavement, African American slaves and Native Americans were dehumanized as godless people. As noted, many African Americans who were enslaved practiced Islam secretly to avoid persecution. Muslims, as well as Jews, were categorized by Christians as groups with the wrong religion and were considered biologically inferior to Christian African slaves who had been Muslim but were forced to convert to Christianity.

Over the last 17 years, the anti-Muslim political spectacle has mushroomed and has resulted in a rise in hate crimes, job discrimination, and bullying incidents in schools as well as opposition to the establishment of mosques across the United States (Greenhouse, 2010). Throughout the years, studies have indicated that discrimination in the workplace has increased by 18% as compared to the previous year. One year after the 9/11 attacks, there were 706 charges filed for discrimination based on the Islamic religion, which is a dramatic increase from the 323 charges of the year prior.

Furthermore, from September 11, 2001, to June 11, 2005, Muslim employees filed more than 2,100 charges of workplace religious discrimination with the Equal Employment Opportunity Commission. The Gallup Center for Muslim Studies (2010) found that 43% of Americans admitted to feeling some prejudice toward Muslims. The study also reported that, compared to Christianity, Judaism, and Buddhism, Islam was the most negatively viewed religion by Americans.

The Department of Justice claimed that between 3,000 and 5,000 hate crimes against Muslims occurred in 2011. The Equal Employment Opportunity Commission received 803 complaints that alleged discrimination from September 2008 to September 2009, a 20% increase from the previous period. In regard to bullying of Muslim children in public schools, to date, there is no national study with statistical information.

However, CAIR California (CAIR-CA) conducted a study on the bullying of Muslim youth. CAIR-CA distributed surveys to 21 counties, in which 471 American Muslim students between the ages of 11 and 18 attended public schools. The largest percentage of surveys completed (30%) came from Orange County, which has a population of 170,000 Muslims, the largest Muslim community in the state.

The survey contained 10 items—the first concerned whether students were comfortable participating in class discussions about Islam or countries where Muslims live. The majority of students reported feeling comfortable, but nearly 20% did not answer positively. The second item focused on whether students felt comfortable letting other students know that they were Muslim and were open to talking about Islam outside the classroom. The majority felt comfortable talking to peers about being Muslim, but 8% did not feel comfortable, and another 8% were undecided.

The third item concerned whether teachers in their school respected their religion. Most of the students responded positively, but nearly 20% did not, and 14% were undecided. The fourth item focused on whether students felt safe at their school. The majority of the students (82%) felt safe, but 4% did not, and 10% were undecided. The fifth was about whether students were ever slapped, kicked, punched, or hit because someone did not like their religion. Although 87% of the students responded they had not experienced physical bullying, more than 10% did report physical bullying (CAIR, 2013).

The sixth item was directed to females who wore hijabs or headscarves and concerned whether they had ever had their hijab tugged or pulled, or were in any way physically violated. Of the girls who wore hijabs, 69% indicated they had not been physically violated, but 17% reported experiencing offensive touching or pulling of their hijab, and 4% reported that they experienced this often or very often. The seventh focused on whether students had ever fielded comments or had rumors spread about them due to their religion.

Half (50%) of the students reported being victims of mean remarks and ignorant rumors because they were Muslim. Students indicated that they had experienced name-calling, such as "Osama Bin Laden" and "terrorist" by their peers. The eighth item was about whether anyone from school made mean or offensive comments about their religion through email, text messages, or social media, such as Facebook or Twitter.

Three-quarters (75%) had never experienced cyberbullying due to their religion; however, 21% responded that they had. The ninth item focused on the reporting of bullying incidents to an adult. Of the students, 32% had reported incidents to their teacher or principal, while 42% had reported incidents to their parents. Finally, the 10th item focused on whether reporting the incident to an adult solved the problem. Fewer than half (42%) responded that reporting the incident helped them, but 26% feared reporting incidents due to the potential for retaliation or losing friends.

CAIR provided a snapshot of what Muslim children and youth are facing in their schools and communities. Muslim Advocates, a national legal advocacy and educational organization, referenced a survey study conducted by Mothers Against Violence in Northern Virginia of 78 Muslim youth. Of the youth, 80% responded they were subjected to bigoted remarks, epithets, and harassment, and 50% reported being called names, including *terrorist*, *raghead*, *tower takers*, and *bomber*, in front of teachers and school administrators.

According to Muslim Advocates (2011), such experiences are the "new reality of growing up Muslim in America today, where one's classmates and teachers wield anti-Muslim attitudes and messages that they learn at school, at home, and from the media."

The marginalization of Muslims as the supposed "Other" in the aftermath of 9/11 and throughout the war on terror has piqued the growth of Muslim-youth leadership as a counter voice and a means to use religious identity to positively engage with diverse groups. American Muslim youth have been encouraged to actively participate in Muslim organizations, such as Muslim student organizations and advocacy organizations. Involvement in such organizations has allowed for outreach efforts, which have given the Muslim community a platform to train the next generation of Muslim leaders.

THE VALUE OF EDUCATION IN ISLAM FOR MUSLIMS

The role of education in Islam is significant and dates back to the origins of Islam, when the angel Gabriel descended from heaven to inform Muhammad of his prophethood. Gabriel commanded Muhammad to read, which Muhammad could not do because he was unlettered. At that point, Gabriel squeezed Muhammad and the prophet began to miraculously recite the revealed verses, later conveying it to his followers for enlightenment and maintenance of the message. Many memorized the Quranic revelations to maintain the Word of God. As articulated by Douglass and Shaikh (2004):

> Education is the first duty of a Muslim, male or female. Knowledge of God is equated with the process of learning and teaching. The well-documented process of preserving Islamic scripture demonstrates the early emergence of a literate tradition and its transmission among Muslims as a social priority. It was incumbent upon the Muslim community from the beginning to commit the words of God and the teachings of Muhammad to memory and to writing.

The teachings of Islam spread across the Arabian Peninsula and beyond into the Far East and Europe. Educational institutions were developed, and Islam flourished in the Arabian Peninsula and abroad. By the early Abbasid period, the literate tradition was available in the humanities and scientific fields and Arabs expanded on their scientific knowledge in seafaring, navigation, astronomy, agriculture, and trade. Formal educational institutions were formed for such learning, some of which still exist today and are among the oldest universities in the world. They include Al-Qarawiyyin in Fez, Al-Nizamiyya in Baghdad, and Al-Azhar in Egypt, among many more in the Middle East and South Asia.

To preserve and nurture their community, the development of educational institutions in America became priority for Muslims. The establishment of the first University of Islam in Detroit, Michigan, afforded African American children the opportunity to attend an institution that emphasized self-knowledge, reliance, and discipline, which filled a need in the African American community. Two years later, the second University of Islam was established in Chicago.

As the NOI evolved as a movement, so did the University of Islam. Rashid and Muhammad (1992) tracked the evolution of the University of Islam into the Sister Clara Muhammad School system it has become today. Historically, the Sister Clara Muhammad Schools were not Islamic schools; they espoused the philosophical underpinnings of the Nation of Islam and were used as institutions to uplift the African American people.

However, as the Islamic validity of NOI's theological tenets were questioned by Sunni Muslims, the schools sought to change the principles and practices that they espoused. The teachings of Sister Clara Muhammad

Schools were made consistent with those of the Quran, and, although the contributions of Africans to civilizations were still emphasized, the religious education was aligned with a more mainstream Islam. Despite these changes, the school still faces the challenge that other Islamic schools face: the establishment of an Islamic educational philosophy that supports a competitive secular academic program.

There are an estimated 400 full-time Islamic schools in the United States and Canada. Islamic schools have formed Muslim educational organizations, such as the Islamic Educators Communications Network (IECN), the Islamic Schools League of America (ISLA), and the Council of Islamic Schools in North America (CISNA). These educational organizations struggle to provide quality secular and religious education to Muslim American children in Islamic schools and to protect Muslim children from suspicion, discrimination, and harassment. The struggle of Islamic schools in a post-9/11 context mimics the struggle of Muslim Americans as a whole: the struggle to be American and simultaneously retain the beliefs and values of Islam (Haddad, Senzai, & Smith, 2009).

PUBLIC EDUCATION

Historically, the character and reputation of teachers, as supposed moral authorities, have been up for public consideration. Although currently to a lesser degree, teachers are still held to a higher moral standard in comparison to other professionals. The negative representation and stereotyping of Muslims in the media as having values antithetical to U.S. values and moral standards have become problematic for Muslim teachers and their workplace relationships.

Case Study One

Brooks (2010) conducted a case study of a Muslim American teacher, Amy, who worked in U.S. public schools, an Islamic school in Georgia, and an Egyptian school to develop a deep understanding of how her religious conversion influenced her workplace relationships.

For the purpose of this study, Amy's experiences only in the United States will be reported. As a convert to Islam who taught in a rural Mississippi school, Amy feared revealing herself, found it difficult to fit in with her fellow teachers and community, and felt limited in her social opportunities. When Amy moved to another public school in a larger town in Mississippi, she revealed that she was a Muslim to her coworkers but felt that her fellow teachers were unknowingly insensitive and ignorant of Islam, and, thus, she did not "connect with other teachers and really didn't feel welcome in the public schools."

After teaching in two public schools in Mississippi, Amy decided to teach at an Islamic school, and she applied to work at a school in Georgia. Amy's experience as a teacher in an American Islamic school in Georgia, however, was very different. She felt a sense of acceptance and quickly became a leader in the school, being one of the few teachers with an official teaching certificate. At this school, Amy found herself in a setting where others shared her religion. She felt a sense of connection to colleagues, the administration, and families.

Based on their shared faith, the Islamic school community helped Amy financially to situate herself in Georgia. As part of her upward mobility at the school, Amy developed strong relationships with students, faculty, and administration. Being accepted into the community gave Amy the feeling of being an "aunt or a second mom" to her students.

She stated that she felt "great responsibility toward them because here the teacher–student relationship extends far beyond a traditional teacher–student relationship that one might have in a public school. It is more like an extended family." Her comfort with her identity as a Muslim allowed her to cultivate her skills and interpersonal relationships at work.

Case Study Two

Newton (2005) provided a nuanced, personal, and multifaceted look at the lived experiences of two Muslim Arab American preservice teachers who worked in New York City post-9/11. Sara worked in a public elementary school and Yasmin, in an Islamic day school. Through artistic mediums such as poetry and graffiti mats, Sara and Yasmin were able to relay intimate classroom experiences and their associated conflicts. Yasmin described her internal struggle in responding to her Palestinian student who said, "Now they know how we feel" (p. 89), referring to Americans in the wake of 9/11. Sara recounted being apprehensive at work and mindful to not "step on anybody's toes, even though they are stepping all over mine" (p. 89).

Case Study Three

Brooks (2014) explored a Muslim teacher's experience in two different types of schools, a public school and an Islamic school, in the southern region of the United States. Natalie, a convert to Islam more than 10 years prior, had been a teacher for several years. Brooks conducted nine semistructured, one-on-one interviews and 16 observations of Natalie's personal and professional life.

The findings showed that Natalie had difficulty fitting into the public school setting, which was composed of 59% Black and 39% White students and staff, and connecting with the school community. She witnessed negative student and teacher interactions, and she was taken aback by how teachers spoke and how they treated students. This school culture made it difficult for her to let staff, students, or parents know that she was Muslim.

Natalie was worried about how they would react to her and that she would be faced with ignorance, indifference, and isolation based on her colleagues' knowing little about Islam. As a result, she avoided revealing her identity to colleagues and students. When Ramadan came, she had to share with her colleagues why she was not eating to end the rumor that she had an eating disorder. Natalie felt that the staff appeared comfortable with her being a Muslim but that they thought that fasting was strange. Natalie concluded that public schools were not as religiously tolerant of their teachers as they expected their teachers to be of students.

In contrast, at the Islamic school, Natalie found herself in a diverse setting, as the students and staff were from a wide range of countries. Upon her arrival, Natalie formed personal and supportive working relationships with colleagues and was accepted by the community. Natalie was comfortable with the attention and support she received and found herself rapidly integrated into the school community, which led her to love her job and be more dedicated to serving.

Based on the study's findings, Brooks emphasized the need for public school leaders to create school cultures that permit religious-minority teachers to experience a positive workplace environment, to identify elements that impede the development of positive workplace relationships, to value and celebrate diversity in their school community by challenging deficit thinking, and, finally, to provide professional development that engages staff in activities and discussions that take them outside of their comfort zones to become more tolerant of diverse culture and religions.

MUSLIM SCHOOL LEADERS

In searching for literature, the researcher came across three studies in education that included school leaders who identified as Muslim but were not specifically chosen for the study because they were Muslim. Halvorsen (2003) conducted a qualitative study on three elementary schools: (a) a public school with students of diverse racial and religious backgrounds and social compositions; (b) a Catholic school; and (c) a public charter school—Southwest Academy—a secular school that caters to a predominantly Muslim community.

Halvorsen's research focused on these three schools' academic approaches to the events of 9/11 and how they handled the one-year commemoration. The Muslim principal included in the study was Mr. Nashif of Southwest Academy. The study captured the immediate post-9/11 challenges that American Muslims experienced in education and gave voice to one American Muslim principal who served in the public school system.

Keval (2012), a South Asian Muslim woman who was born and raised in Kenya, conducted an analytic autoethnographic study that highlighted her leadership practices as a principal in an urban school with more than 1,200 students of high poverty. Although her study did not focus on her ethnic, racial, or religious background, it did present who she is as a person and the experiences that molded her as an educational leader.

Davidson (2011) recounts the experiences and leadership struggles of the author, Dr. Debbie Almontaser, as an American Muslim school principal related to the founding of the Khalil Gibran International Academy in New York. In addition, two articles recount the author's experiences. That focused on her attempt in organizing a campaign that emerged in support of the Khalil Gibran Academy, whereby a coalition of Arab, Muslim, Jewish, immigrant, labor, and peace groups engaged in widespread outreach and launched a media campaign in defense of the school and its principal.

The researcher also chronicled the author's relationship with the Jewish community before and after the smear campaign that forced her out of her position, the interests of individuals and organizations on both sides of the controversy, and what could have been done differently to maintain good relations. Accounts were also provided of the anti-Arab and anti-Muslim hysteria that evolved after the founding of the Khalil Gibran International Academy.

To date, the personal experience of the author seems to be the only one of an American Muslim principal that is documented and relays that global events, political discourse, and the media coverage of Islam and Muslims have had an impact on the author's leadership at a public school. Thus, there is a clear need to conduct further research on the lived experiences of American Muslim principals.

This chapter has offered readers with a framework to understand the history and current state of American Muslims, along with a background of the reasoning for the study and its conducted research. With this knowledge, readers will now delve into the methodology of the research, providing them with details of the study approach and the participants.

KEY CHAPTER FINDINGS

- Researchers note that there is not enough minority presence in principalship. In a study conducted from 2003 to 2004, it was found that only 17.6% of principals in the United States were of minority background.

- African American leadership literature is present, though it mostly centers around urban leaders and is conducted by those not a part of the African American community.
- Islam in America dates back to the slave trade, continuing through the formation of the Nation of Islam and arrival of immigrant communities.
- It is important to note that Muslim American women are the most highly educated groups in America, following Jewish American women.
- The events of 9/11 gradually led to developments in Islamophobia, prejudice, and bullying.

Chapter Four

How This Study Was Conducted

Fourteen individuals participated in this study, composed of male and female American Muslim principals who serve in public and charter schools.

Prior to delving into the findings and substance of the research, it is imperative to frame how this particular study was conducted. As noted in the prior chapter, the study's main purpose is to explore the lived experiences of American Muslim principals who are currently serving or have served in public schools post-9/11.

The study of the lived experiences would determine how global events, political discourse, and the media coverage of Islam and Muslims are having an impact on their leadership and spirituality. In order to fully understand the intention of the study, a set of five research questions was created to assess the subject matter from all possible angles:

1. How is the performance of American Muslim principals affected by their religion?
2. How do American Muslim principals perceive their treatment as compared to that of their non-Muslim colleagues in their district, in their relations with their staff, students, parents, and their school community at large?
3. How do American Muslim principals perceive that non-Muslims view them?
4. How are the challenges that American Muslim principals face different from those of their non-Muslim colleagues?
5. How is the spirituality of American Muslim principals affected by their leadership in a public school setting?

METHODOLOGY

A phenomenological qualitative methodology was used to draw out the lived experiences of participants, or in simpler terms, the conduction of interviews enabled the researcher to best obtain detailed descriptions of experiences. Interviews are often described as one of the most effective methodologies in attempting to delve into inner experiences unprobed in everyday life. It is useful to use when the researcher has identified a phenomenon to understand, and has individuals who can provide a description of what they have experienced.

The two questions of "how" and "what" is experienced provide a concrete framework for asking questions and recording answers. The fact that this approach relies on individual experiences means that the stories to be told will be told from the participants' voices and not those of the researcher. The outcome sought in this particular endeavor was to unearth the meaning and essences of the lived experience of American Muslim principals through rich, in-depth, descriptive, and interpretive information that promotes a comprehensive understanding of the phenomenon being studied.

The approach taken for this particular study was the transcendental phenomenological, which essentially provides the researcher with a systematic approach to analyze data about the lived experiences of participants. This particular approach requires that the researcher, in this case the author, identify and acknowledge one's own experience and position related to the study before undertaking the project. An approach of this manner allows for an easier study of the realities of the natural world to be examined, void of biases.

The researcher found 20 American Muslims leaders nationally; however, 14 of those individuals participated in the study, composed of male and female American Muslim principals who serve in public and charter schools. The participants included principals who have served pre- and post-9/11. Given the diversity of the American Muslim community, it was intended to find participants reflective of this reality.

All participants were identified and recruited by the researcher. An email was sent via the national listservs of American Muslim organizations and networks that introduced the study and invited prospective participants to participate as well as requested further distribution of the email to friends and colleagues. This is known as a snowball sampling method, which is considered to be the most widely employed method in social sciences qualitative research.

The participants hailed from four regions of the United States: Northeast, South, Midwest, and West, including eight females and six males from diverse racial and ethnic backgrounds (Figure 4.1). They were or remain as principals at the elementary, middle, and high school levels. Of the 14 participants, nine were U.S. born, three were born in the Middle East, one was born in Pakistan, and another was born in Tanzania. Of the U.S.-born principals, six were African Americans, and three were Arab Americans (Figure 4.2).

Their years of experience as principal ranged from one to over 15 years. Within the prior five years, one participant retired to raise her grandchildren, one participant began work as an education consultant, one began work in youth leadership development in the private sector, and one began work as a trainer in principal leadership in the Middle East. Of the 14 principals, two led publicly funded charter schools. Three of the 14 principals lead schools that are full-fledged public schools, with 90% of their students being Muslim and their staff being predominantly White.

The rest led, or have led, schools composed largely of African American students, followed by Hispanic students and a small number of English language learners. Three participants led K–5 elementary schools, while six led K–8 schools; one led a middle school, and four led high schools (Figure 4.3).

Although the study consisted of 14 participants, four of the case studies will be featured more prevalently than the 10 other participants in this book for a closer look at their lived experiences. All participants were assigned

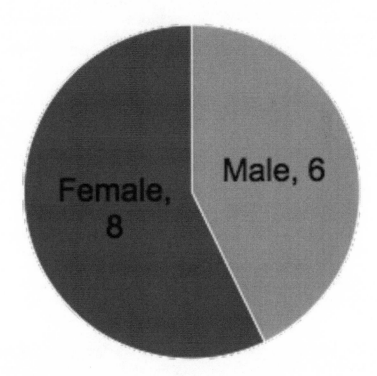

Figure 4.1. Breakdown of Participants: Female and Male

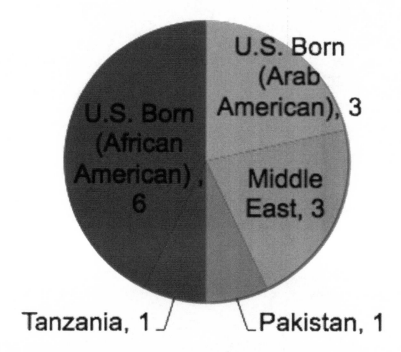

Figure 4.2. Participant Place of Birth

pseudonyms to protect their identities. The four participants represent significant themes that were discovered throughout the research process, and each one offers a unique perspective to the study as well.

RESEARCH COMPLIANCE

In compliance with the ethical requirements of questioning from the Institutional Review Board, all matters were adhered to. The participants received a study orientation packet electronically as a means to fully understand the research study and its risks and potential. All participants were given the option to accept or decline the opportunity to participate in the study.

If they accepted, they were obligated to complete an informed consent agreement. They were informed that even if they agreed to participate, they would have the option to withdraw at any time for any reason. They also were informed that no compensation would be made for their participation in the study.

Because there are so few American Muslim principals who serve in U.S. public schools, the possibility of participants' being identified and/or associated with comments made during the interviews was a concern. To ensure

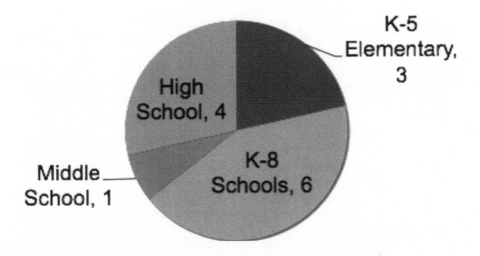

Figure 4.3. Participant Leadership School Level

that this did not happen, participants had their identity and privacy protected before, during, and after the study to the fullest extent possible, and they were informed of this protection. As part of this assurance, all participants and their schools were assigned pseudonyms to protect their identities and privacy.

FOUR CASE STUDIES

Najla, a female Arab American participant, started her education career as a public school teacher who wore the hijab, known as the Muslim head covering. Throughout her professional career, Najla gradually worked toward a higher position of principalship. She served as an assistant principal for four years and soon after became a principal of a large elementary school that had been experiencing functional difficulties. During her interviews, Najla reflected that her experiences post-9/11 significantly affected her outlook on living as a Muslim in America and working as a professional, leading her to remove her hijab, headscarf.

Rula, a female of South Asian background, started her career as a teacher, then guidance counselor, followed by positions of school leadership. Her particular story highlights the effect that 9/11 had on her work environment and coworkers, leading to traumatic experiences that resulted in her removal from her position and severe health issues and psychological distress.

Aziz, an African American male principal, offered further insight into troubling experiences with coworkers and his overall work environment.

Furthermore, Aziz shared valuable views from a racial perspective, as he reflected on his position as not only a Muslim American, but also an African American. He addressed the question of both religion and race playing a role in how he is perceived and lives on a day-to-day basis.

The final participant that will be examined in detail is Aiman, who has a particularly unique background. Aiman grew up in Pakistan for a large portion of his life and moved to the United States for pursuit of greater professional opportunity and family. He serves as a principal at a school in a prominent metropolitan area. His understanding of Islam and Muslims has been shaped by his experiences growing up around those from other countries who gave him, in what he describes, a very unfortunate and frustrating view of the religion. Aiman does not strongly identify as a practicing Muslim, though he does embrace his Muslim identity. His story offers a unique look into leadership as a Muslim in America, although not necessarily American himself.

TIME FRAME OF STUDY

The interviews with the 14 participants began in August 2015 and ended in March 2016, with the backdrop of global events and political discourse during that time period. The political climate for American Muslims and those perceived to be Muslims was ripe with incidents indicative of Islamophobia and national tragedies due to terrorist attacks.

The year 2015 began with the *Charlie Hebdo* terror attacks in Paris and ended with the San Bernardino shooting. These events led to 71 mosque incidents that included vandalism, threats, desecration of Quranic texts, pig heads left outside entrances, targeting with bullets, and fire bombings, resulting in the highest ever recorded number of incidents against Muslims, according to a CAIR (2015) report.

The execution-style murder of three Muslim students in Chapel Hill, North Carolina, the hate crime shooting of a Muslim cabdriver in Pittsburgh, the beating of a teenager in Seattle who was thrown off a rooftop, and other incidents resulted in a total of nine murders from December 2014 to December 2015 in the United States and Canada.

A total of 52 personal assaults and threats against American Muslims across the United States from November 2014 to July 2015 were reported. This total, however, likely underestimates the actual number of assaults, as many American Muslims do not report hate crimes to law enforcement (Bridge Initiative Team, 2015b). Based on FBI statistics, the average number per month of suspected hate crimes against Muslims in 2015 was 12.6 (Lichtblau, 2015).

Additional incidents that display traces of anti-Muslim behavior include the arrest of a high school student suspected by his school of bringing a bomb to school after creating a homemade clock (Contrera, 2015), the closing of Virginia schools after parental outrage about the teaching of Islam (Brumfield, 2015), and the removal of a Muslim teacher for showing the movie about the Nobel Prize winner Malala Yousafzai (Deak, 2015).

Most recently, the 2016 presidential campaign had included a large commentary on anti-Muslim rhetoric. The Republican Party front-runner Donald Trump called for a "Muslim ban," and former candidate Ben Carson announced that Muslims should not be permitted to become president. While the candidates did attempt to refine their remarks to suggest that they were speaking of terrorists who were Muslim, the initial comments made impacted Muslim American perceptions of their identity in the United States. During the past 14 years, Muslims and the rest of the world have experienced political spectacle that has been orchestrated by Al-Qaeda, ISIS, interest groups, GOP political candidates, and the media.

DATA COLLECTION

Research data was collected through the use of multiple in-depth interviews, field notes, and other documents such as the preinterview questionnaires. A preinterview questionnaire was sent to every participant to elicit demographic information as well as written responses to the interview questions. Two interviews were then conducted with each participant. During the in-person interviews, the researcher took field notes to record body language or other factors that could not be captured by the recording.

The first interview was conducted in person, lasted between 20 and 30 minutes, and was audio recorded. This interview was driven by the following carefully developed interview questions asked of all participants in the first interview:

1. As an American Muslim principal who serves in a public school, have you been publicly open about being Muslim within your school community?
2. What was your reaction to the September 11th events?
3. As an American Muslim principal, how would you describe the social climate in your community in the aftermath of 9/11 for you and other Muslims?
4. What is the current social climate in your community? Is it the same as after 9/11, or has it changed? Please explain.
5. How do global events (terrorist attacks) committed by people who call themselves Muslim make you, as an American Muslim principal, feel?

6. How does the ongoing political discourse about Islam and Muslims make you, as an American Muslim principal, feel?
7. How does the media coverage of Islam and Muslims make you, as an American Muslim principal, feel?
8. As an American Muslim principal, are you comfortable engaging in discussions about Islam and Muslims with members of your school community who are not Muslim?
9. As an American Muslim principal, are you comfortable with exhibiting your faith physically in dress and behavior?
10. As an American Muslim principal, do you fear that being open and practicing your religion will affect your leadership and spirituality?

The second interview was a follow-up via Skype and/or telephone, which was also recorded and transcribed. The second interview was driven by the following probing questions:

1. As a school principal and thinking about your duties as a school leader, do you feel that you have the responsibility to clear up misconceptions and stereotypes about Muslims, or any minority group for that matter, which may be prevalent today?
2. In context of you being the principal of your school and global events and crises that occur. Can you share if and how you as principal and your school dealt with the aftermath?
3. Do you ever feel that you experience unique challenges being a Muslim principal compared to other staff members who are not Muslim?
4. Have there ever been any conflicts or conversations where you felt your Muslim identity was being challenged or questioned? By colleagues, families, or school boards?
5. Do you think the current global and political climate has an effect on American Muslim leaders serving the public school communities? Or an effect on their psychology?
6. How often do you think you concern yourself with political correctness as a Muslim principal in your school?
7. On a scale of 1–10, how heavy of a role do you believe your faith played in the everyday stress and pressures of your job as principal?
8. What challenges do you think, if any, American Muslim school principals and leaders face, in light of the current social and political climate in this country?
9. For you and other principals who openly identify as American Muslims, do you feel there is any need for programming, organizations, or forums catering to your demographic or the issues you think are prevalent?

10. You've had some time to reflect on the questions and discussion we had from the previous interview. Is there anything else you want to mention about your experience and perspective, that you did not have a chance to share before?

DATA ANALYSIS

The primary strategy for the findings of this study was the analysis of the data from the preinterview questionnaires, the recorded interview transcripts, and impressions formed from direct contact with participants. The findings were analyzed for categories and themes. The data was grouped by relevant text, and repeating ideas and themes were noted. The participants' transcribed interviews were to be read and reread to develop a feeling for their experiences and to make sense of their account. This was examined through the lens of the theoretical framework, political spectacle theory.

Political spectacle is a theory that was pioneered by political scientist Murray Edelman. The theory of political spectacle identifies how social situations, leaders, and enemies are constructed to create political spectacle. Political spectacle is a construction of symbolic threats that misinform the public to legitimize political action and reify inequalities. Within each spectacle, an issue or a policy is purposely misrepresented to the advantage of one party over the other, whether be it politicians, researchers, the mass media, or the corporate world.

Edelman (1988) emphasized political spectacle as a construction and a process by which political elites and groups keep the public passive. Through the dissemination and manipulation of particular symbols and messages, powerful groups are able to effectively conceal and distract the public from their privileged political positions.

Edelman (1985, 1988) theorized that this use of spectacle not only successfully keeps the appearances of political elites intact but also distracts the public from its ability to engage in reasoned discourse about the real problematic social situations that face society. Through this process, a poorly informed public is given the impression that they are rationally reacting to facts and political news. Edelman (1988) reversed this flow of information and, through the treatment of political developments as constructions, sought to account for these political events through how they are observed and interpreted by people.

While examining the data through a political spectacle theory lens, significant accounts were extracted, that is, statements that pertain directly to the phenomenon being examined, and meanings were formulated for these significant accounts and statements. The formulations illuminate the meanings veiled in the various contexts of the phenomenon of political spectacle. The formulated meanings were then categorized into clusters of themes that are common to all participants. It was then compared to the original transcriptions for validation and for confirming consistency between the emerging conclusions and the participants' original stories.

Following the categorization of themes, the findings were then integrated into an exhaustive analysis and comparison. Following a comprehensive analysis, some participants were contacted again to determine their position on the findings and to offer any new perspective or changes. Throughout the entire process, field notes were also analyzed and all findings were discussed with advisors and colleagues who are considered to be experts in the area of study.

As the sole researcher who facilitated the interview process and analyzed the data, the researcher abided by the research code of ethics at all times and was impartial throughout the research process. She took the necessary steps to avoid unduly influencing the results of the study to the best of her ability.

The researcher continually self-checked as she proceeded with the interviews to refrain from making biased comments, asking one-sided questions, and using leading or probing questions based on personal experience or attitudes that she may have subconsciously held. The researcher also wrote memos throughout the data collection and analysis as a way to continually examine and reflect upon her engagement with the participants and data to maintain objectivity.

The participants from New York City public schools, which is where the researcher served as a principal, may have been hesitant to answer questions honestly for fear of retribution or may subconsciously have thought that the New York City Public School System administration would be aware of their responses. Participants were assured that their interviews would remain confidential and that their identities would never be released. To capture the perceptions of these participants' lived experiences, the study employed the two perspectives of phenomenological analysis noted by Creswell (2005): those of the participants who are actually living through the phenomenon and that of the researcher who has an interest in the identified phenomena.

The author's position and standing was noted in regard to the study of American Muslim principals of public schools. As the sole researcher, the author shared her personal story, understandings, past knowledge, and assumptions based on her experiences. In going forward with this research study, she set aside her biases and preconceived judgments and aimed to maintain a fair balance between subjectivity and objectivity (Moustakas, 1994).

As the methodology of this study has been presented, readers are now able to understand the research that will be presented to them in the following four chapters regarding the themes that were discovered in relation to the American Muslim principals' experience post-9/11. The themes that will be examined in depth will focus on political climate, role of the media, being seen as an inferior and the "Other," unconscious fear, spirituality, and education and community over spectacle, along with other additional thoughts.

KEY CHAPTER IDEAS

- To explore the lived experiences of American Muslim principals who are currently serving or have served in public schools post-9/11, a set of five research questions were developed:

  - How is the performance of American Muslim principals affected by their religion?
  - How do American Muslim principals perceive their treatment as compared to that of their non-Muslim colleagues in their district, in their relations with their staff, students, parents, and their school community at large?
  - How do American Muslim principals perceive that non-Muslims view them?
  - How are the challenges that American Muslim principals face different from those of their non-Muslim colleagues?
  - How is the spirituality of American Muslim principals affected by their leadership in a public school setting?

- Fourteen individuals participated in the study, composed of male and female American Muslim principals who serve in public and charter schools. The participants included principals who have served pre- and post-9/11.
- To ensure privacy protection, all participants and their schools were assigned pseudonyms to protect their identities.
- The following four participants will be examined in depth for this publication: Najla, Rula, Aziz, and Aiman.
- The interviews with the participants began in August 2015 and ended in March 2016, with the backdrop of global events and political discourse during that time period.
- Research data was collected through the use of multiple in-depth interviews, field notes, and other documents such as the preinterview questionnaires.
- All research was examined through the lens of the framework of political spectacle theory.

Chapter Five

Political Climate and Role of the Media

We live in an age of perpetual media feeds—so that keeps me in a state of red alert.

IN THE CONTEXT OF POLITICAL SPECTACLE THEORY

In examining the role of political climate, gaining a better sense of the theory of political spectacle, which was the lens used to analyze the data in this study, may be beneficial for the reader. Pioneered by political scientist Murray Edelman, the theory of political spectacle identifies how social situations, leaders, and enemies are constructed to create political spectacle.

The theory of political spectacle comprises symbolic threats that provide the public with misinformation as a means to legitimize political action and reify inequalities. An issue or policy can be purposefully misrepresented to the advantage of one party over another. Edelman theorized that this political spectacle usage would essentially distract the public from their ability to engage in reasonable discussions about social issues. And it is this process that leads to a poorly informed public believing that they are rationally reacting to political news.

To understand why political spectacle is the appropriate theoretical framework for this study, the role of the principal must be defined in the context of the theory. A principal is a public figure whose constituents are the school staff, students, families, and the neighboring community. Principals are regarded as leaders and actors in the lives of the people whom they serve. They have philosophical and ideological beliefs that are shaped by their morals and values that permeate their leadership.

Principals are appointed and employed by a board and serve at the discretion of their superintendent. They are bound by institutional rules that are similar to those of elected officials. Society at large holds principals to a higher standard than that of other leaders because they are entrusted with the lives of children in the K–12 setting, and they are held accountable for their actions 24 hours a day, seven days a week. For example, an incident such as a simple argument with a neighbor can result in police action and negative press (Weaver, 2007).

Principals lead with a mission and vision and are seen as role models who are praised or criticized depending on their interactions with staff, students, parents, and the community. The role of a principal is political in nature. According to Edelman (1988):

> People involved in politics are symbols to other observers: they stand for ideologies, values, or moral stances and they become role models, benchmarks, or symbols of threat and evil. . . . Leaders are ready symbols of good or evil, while historical trends, social conditions, relations of production, and modes of discourse are not. Leaders become objectifications of whatever worries or pleases observers of the political scene because it is easy to identity with them, support or oppose them, love or hate them.

POLITICAL SPECTACLE IN K–12 EDUCATION

The role of political spectacle may be present in different forms and various realms. Within the field of education, political spectacle has played out frequently. Education policy programs, in particular, have become the symbolic site for intervention on the part of politicians to gain political advantage. This forged relationship between politics and policy has prompted research on the ways that policies in cultural and social institutions serve political propaganda (Miller-Kahn & Smith, 2001).

While higher education policy may seem to be the more common area of influence, political spectacle has also proven to impact the field of K–12 education. Anderson (2007) discusses the mechanisms through which spectacle is assembled, with a particular focus on the role of the media in school-reform policies and practices and the increasing role that media plays in contemporary educational politics. Anderson claims that, in addition to the media's informing and promoting certain social agendas, the role of the media in influencing education politics and policy has intensified.

Miller-Kahn and Smith (2001) studied the role of interest groups in influencing school policies in a Boulder, Colorado, school district and showed how school choice was introduced as a solution to the problem of under-achieving schools as a means to divert public funds for private use. Their case study highlighted how, through the construction of spectacle, the audience (in this case, parents) were given the illusion of increasing their decision-making opportunities when, in fact, this was not the case.

Interest groups presented choice policy as associated with free-market principles and liberalism to convince parents that school choice was a means through which parents could win control over the schools and have a specialized and more involved role in their children's educational lives. However, the inherent exclusion of certain students from educational opportunities and the political opportunities that were being created were kept concealed. In this way, political spectacle hinders democracy.

Another example of political spectacle in education policy concerns the case of bilingual education policy (Proposition 203) in Arizona. According to Wright (2005), the implementation of Proposition 203 was the result of political spectacle, not of rational policy decision making. As a result of its passage, restrictions were placed on bilingual and ESL (English as a second language) programs, and an English-only education system was mandated. According to Wright, the Proposition 203 campaign employed all the tactics involved in constructing a spectacle.

Through the use of symbolic political language, the campaign was given the title English for the Children, or the Unz initiative. According to Wright, the invocation of children in the title masked the involvement of the California political hopeful Ron Unz, who not only authored the proposition but also was its financial backer. Wright feels that Unz's involvement as an outside policy actor with personal gains to implement Proposition 203 was masked. This was another case in which attempts at democratic policy making were subverted through biased research, sound bites, policy actors, and the naming of heroes and enemies (Wright, 2005).

In a similar vein, Koyama and Bartlett (2011) explored bilingual education policy in the context of New York City schools. Koyama and Bartlett studied a successful bilingual school and the ways in which educational actors were taken in by educational policies at both federal and district local levels, specifically how the assessment policies imposed on the individual school became a vehicle through which the Bloomberg (city) and Bush (federal) administrations benefited.

POLITICAL CLIMATE

With the backdrop of political spectacle in mind, the first major theme found through the research, political climate, will be discussed. Political climate serves as a significant influence on the experience of Muslims in America, especially following the events of 9/11. A climate that is ripe with fear and hysteria generates notions of anxiety and, as will be discussed, can have a severe impact on an individual's mental health and well-being. Over the past 15 years, the world has experienced a political climate filled with spectacle

that has been orchestrated by Al-Qaeda, ISIS, neoconservatives, white su-
premacists, Republican political candidates, and the media.

This began with the coverage of 9/11, which was captured in a 24-hour
news cycle on CNN and other cable networks. The participants of this study
raised concern about the political climate from the time immediately after
9/11 to the present time of the study. All 14 participants clearly indicated that
political spectacle played a role in perpetuating political discourse and amplifying global events, and that the political climate played a pivotal role in
the way that Islam and Muslims are portrayed.

Participants recounted their experiences in the moments after 9/11 and
discussed how the global perspective dramatically changed for Muslims
around the world and for themselves. Due in part to the war on terror, safety
became a huge concern for individuals and institutions across the United
States. During the Bush administration in 2002, the Department of Homeland
Security developed the "Homeland Security Advisory System" to alert
Americans of potential risks of terrorism.

The system consisted of five color-coded levels, from green to blue to
yellow to orange to red, with each successive color indicating a higher threat
of terrorism (Robinson, 2011). Such a system created a heightened sense of
awareness of the presence of American Muslims, especially while traveling
and essentially posing a "threat" to American safety.

All 14 participants drew attention to the 2016 presidential candidates,
namely, Donald Trump and Ben Carson, who they believed used the Republican platform to fearmonger Islam and Muslims. Each one of the participants was chilled by Trump's proposal to ban Muslims and by the endorse-
ment that he received from the Ku Klux Klan (KKK). In response to Trump's
comments about Muslims, the KKK distributed flyers in the South to cleanse
the United States of Muslims (Lauten, 2015). One participant, Aziz, stated
that as a result of Trump's rhetoric, he had a desire to seek dual citizenship
for reasons of safety:

> I think that if Trump becomes the president it might be time to get dual
> citizenship somewhere because America's going down the deep end, a dark
> road, because we're fascinated with personalities as opposed to morals and
> values and specific issues. And that's a problem. And it makes our job a little
> bit more difficult just being a principal, getting our children to think critically,
> because they're exposed to so much pop culture which feeds them the worst
> part of themselves, which is problematic.

The discussion on political climate also had a significant effect on the
participants' psyche, leading them to develop serious fears and concerns.
Rula, a principal with a South Asian background, started her career as a
teacher. She later became a guidance counselor and then pursued school
leadership. Rula, reflecting on her own experience, shared deep insights into

the psychological impact the political climate may potentially have on an individual:

> I've often considered [this point] because how we feel socially and emotional-
> ly, psychologically, is going to impact what we deliver. And as a leader you
> have to be able to think freely. You have to be able to have space for innova-
> tion and in the current political climate, it's like you have to question yourself.
> And I'll give you a specific example that like if you want to present a certain
> idea, you're going to double check with yourself that if it's going to look a
> certain way, and how is this going to sound. Because you don't want to sound
> a certain way, you know. I don't know how to describe it, but it's like you'll
> almost have to vet yourself before you bring any ideas to your staff or to your
> school community, because in addition to just the idea being evaluated when
> you present it, you also know that you as a person with your identity as a
> Muslim, are being evaluated.

The impact of the discourse was not only mentioned in the context of leadership, but also concerning students of the school communities the principals
were a part of. Several participants expressed direct concern for the Muslim
students of their schools, stating that they feared students developing inse-
cure personalities that shy away from their identities.

A list of prevalent terms came up as well that were commonly mentioned
throughout the interviews, including "discouraged," "insulting," "burden-
some to apologize," "frustrating," "ignorance," "numb," "heightened sense
of personal responsibility," and "the dumbing down of America." Most participants also acknowledged that the political climate has an effect on their
leadership and how they interact with others. Najla described how she felt on
the day of the 9/11 terrorist attacks:

> The TV was on in the auditorium, and several teachers were around it, and I
> walked by, and I was like, what's going on? They didn't talk to me. Not one
> person told me what was going on. They just kind of looked at me up and
> down, and they were crying, looking at me as if I was at fault, immediately.
> I'm like, what's going on? And then they said to me, "Some Arab Americans
> took a plane into a building." . . . It was a Muslim, and people weren't talking
> to me. And friends whom I knew weren't talking to me. So I isolated [myself
> in] my classroom, and I remember crying, and I went underneath my desk
> because I was so shaken by everything.

In 2005, Najla decided to take off her hijab due to her feeling isolated, the
surrounding climate, and the pressure that she was receiving from her family
to ensure her safety. That same year, Najla began her administration program, which she completed in 2007, and was appointed as an assistant principal at a different school. At the school, she told no one that she was a Muslim

unless she was asked. This may have also resulted from a sense of powerlessness that she developed post-9/11:

> It actually happened to my husband and I when we were in Canada and we were asked to step out of our car. And our cars were searched and we were asked questions separately—right after September 11—because I was wearing a hijab. You feel hopeless—not hopeless—you feel, how do you say, powerless, right? Because they're going to do what they need to do to protect the country, right? You can't blame them. You can't say, oh, this is wrong. In your heart of hearts you know that they're only pulling me over because of my husband's surname, Salaam, and my hijab but you have to do what you have to do to protect the country.

Rula shared telling details of her experience of the aftermath of 9/11:

> Once it was declared in the media that "radical Muslims" were behind the attack, I knew that a wave of Islamophobia would ripple through the world. I wear a hijab, so I knew that I would be personification of the "enemy" for quite a lot of folks. Of course, it wasn't fair. It just was the new reality that I had to face. Although most coworkers were respectful, some made insensitive, somewhat ignorant comments. A few examples [of both types of comments were]: "I know that most Muslims are good, like you. . . . I'm glad that you're not a radical or extremist"; "What does your community know about bin Laden?"; "You're very brave to return to work right after [the attacks]." This [last comment] was said by a district administrator who was at my school campus on September 12 to train all guidance counselors for crisis intervention.
>
> The local mosque [the Muslim Center of New York in Flushing, Queens] was assigned an NYPD squad car in case there was any retaliation. So those of us who attended prayer services there were greeted by NYPD officers. Very few people attended prayers at the masjid [mosque] at that time, perhaps out of fear. Many Muslim friends canceled social events because they did not want to give the appearance that Muslims were celebrating.

As seen through Rula's narration, many American Muslims predicted that the climate of political spectacle would lead to the concept of "personification of the enemy."

Participants who were of African American descent mentioned that they had developed perceptions that their religious identity had often trumped their ethnic or racial identity. They claimed African American Muslims were also seen as serious threats to the national community, despite the fact that none of the 9/11 terrorists were of African American descent. They were no longer disassociated from terrorism but, in fact, seen as a potential threat. As a result of 9/11 and other attacks that followed, race and ethnicity were trumped by religious identity due to political spectacle that created the climate in which there was an association of African American Muslims with potential terrorism.

Aziz, who is an African American, reflected on his experience in relation to race. He claimed to present himself as an ordinary, well-dressed African American man but felt that when his name is uttered, his Muslim identity is the only aspect that is focused on. Regarding his identity contemplation, Aziz stated:

> This feeling of, how were they looking at me? What's their perception of me? Should I wear my kufi? How is this going to impact my son and my [other] children? How am I viewed? I even had one of my friends who shared with me, because she was a nurse, that a doctor said, "He's a Muslim," and she had to kind of tell him that, you know, he's not what you believe he is . . . just this whole perception of who you are, and people hearing your last name and having particular prejudgment or prejudice against you. So that's what I was feeling.

Not all participants, however, expressed that their work performance or professional life was necessarily affected by the climate, even though they perceived the political discourse was problematic. In the case of Aiman, a principal with a South Asian background who grew up in Pakistan and had a particularly unique upbringing, he found the discourse to be comedic in a sense:

> I am American. I am a US citizen. But if two clowns like Donald Trump and Ben Carson are going to be the frontrunners of a political party that that goes to show sort of, I mean, you know, it's embarrassing. It's just embarrassing, not just because of their stance on Muslims but their stance on Hispanics and Latinos and yeah, they're just idiots. It's entertainment. I turn it on, I watch it, I'm extremely on the liberal side of things, but I love watching Ben Carson and Donald Trump because it sounds like, it seems like a comedy show to me. I think that there are people in this country who take them seriously which is an unfortunate and poor reflection of the level of introspection and education of people in this country, but it is what it is, and knowledge about different things, things that are not American, and that's, I guess, part of what I was saying earlier is that the fear is not, as much, I see, of Muslim, but anything that Americans don't know. Does it affect my work? No. Idiots like Ben Carson and Trump are the last thing that hopefully will affect my work.

It is worth noting that in every interview that was conducted, a heavy discussion surrounding political discourse occurred. Throughout the interviews, any mention of political climate was overwhelmingly focused on 9/11 and the days that followed to the time of the interview. Every participant offered reflections on the political climate, which they believe played a strong role in the way Islam and Muslims are portrayed and perceived. Participants also acknowledged that the political climate has an effect on their leadership and how they interact with others. Another factor that directly ties in with political climate is the role of the media, which also has implications on the leadership and spirituality of the participants.

ROLE OF THE MEDIA

Every participant addressed the role of the media in discussing 9/11 and all events following. They also expressed negative views on the media portrayal of Muslims and Islam. The word used most widely by the participants during the interviews was "media," which appeared 143 times throughout all transcripts and documents, excluding the interviewer's use of the term.

The term *media* encapsulates a broad range of mediums including print; online papers; blogs; social media, such as Facebook and Twitter; and radio and cable networks, such as CNN, NBC, ABC, CBS, PBS, and Fox. In a follow-up question that requested clarification from all participants in regard to understanding of the term *media*, the majority stated that they were referring to cable networks, such as CNN, ABC, and Fox.

Every participant in the study believed that media coverage hypostatized political spectacle created by forces such as Al-Qaeda, the Islamophobia industry (anti-Muslim interest groups/individuals), politicians, ISIS, and GOP presidential candidates regarding the way Islam and Muslims are portrayed and perceived (Ali et al., 2011). Participants connected the media to the "dehumanization of Muslims" and "becoming desensitized," associating it with "distrust" and "distorting images."

Participants also labeled the media as "biased and divisive" and the "source of all troubles." All participants also indicated a lack of confidence in the U.S. media. They collectively believed that some media outlets, particularly FOX and CNN, propagated fear and hate through their unfavorable portrayal of American Muslims.

The media hypnosis post-9/11, as one participant described it, leads people to "live by the media." This speaks to Edelman's theory of political spectacle, as described by Miller-Kahn and Smith (2001), which casts political actors as leaders, allies, and enemies whose roles are socially constructed by interest groups and society as well as by the media. These political actors use symbolic language to mesmerize their audiences, and, according to Edelman (1985), symbolic language is developed to create mental images in the mind of stakeholders who are being sought in an effort to be won over.

Aziz described the media as

> promoting ignorance, promoting the boogieman. America always has to have a boogieman. Besides, I'm a Muslim principal, or I'm a Muslim teacher. America historically has to have a boogieman, so people can rally against him and really be psychologically swayed to think certain ways. So, you know, there's

a dumbing down of America. They've dumbed down America. They do it through these sound bites and these individuals who really have no political science background or personalities, and they promote that to espouse certain ideas that really promote disunity amongst us all. But I think that's the intent because if we really start to look at what's really going on, you'll find that we'd be dissatisfied more than satisfied. So I think it's designed to do that. And if people can't read in between the lines and be critical and analytical thinkers, they're going to believe whatever they hear, no matter what news media promotes it. I think it's dangerous.

Rula related how media coverage makes her feel, explaining that it creates an "us" versus "them" state of red-alert dichotomy that sends chills through the American Muslim communities:

It makes me feel like entire rolls of media footage, war photographs, YouTube videos of hooded ISIS soldiers, etc., enter the room with me—that I have a neon sign floating above my head that lists all the horrible world events caused by criminals and miscreants posing as Muslims.

It directly impacts the way that my fellow Americans, my colleagues, staff, students see me. We live in an age of perpetual media feeds: news, opinion, propaganda, talking heads, and political candidates espousing banishment of Muslims. So that keeps me in a state of red alert. Most Muslims that I talk to, especially Muslim women who wear the hijab, feel that there is a target on our backs. So that kind of sideways societal gaze feeds into how I may be perceived as an American Muslim principal. I'm under a microscope; small actions will undoubtedly have ripple effects. Molehills will become mountains. A harmless comment CAN lead to something seen as suspicious or radical. I know that if a non-Muslim administrator at my school makes an off-color remark about bombs, she will make a room of people laugh with her. Now, what do you think will happen if I do it?

When asked about the media in particular, Aiman expressed his opinion that governmental influence plays a role in the coverage:

Yes, right now, there is Islamophobia, and it's soon to be replaced by China-phobia or Indiaphobia, any of the above, whenever the State Department decides that it's time for CNN and MSNBC and Fox News to start focusing their attention on some other rival that they want to use to unite the people in the United States and [cause a] mind shift.

It is important to note the role that right-wing media plays into the experience of American Muslim principals. Right-leaning groups such as Jihad Watch express more openly negative opinions of Islam and Muslims, often attacking American Muslim organizations and leaders for secretly infusing Islamic ideals and Shariah law into everyday American life. Jihad Watch, for example, was the first group that brought the story of this author to light in the media, which led other media organizations to follow suit.

Participants during their follow-up interviews were asked whether they felt an organization catering to American Muslim school leaders would be beneficial, for the purpose of dialogue, support, and the exchanging of ideas. Most participants expressed positive reactions to the idea, with the exception of two showing signs of reservation. The main reason for the hesitation to potentially join such a group centered on the concern of government surveillance and the attack of right-wing media groups. It is interesting to note that the power of the right-wing media was the primary reason for one of the participants not involving himself in the idea:

> I can just imagine Jihad Watch just latching onto this and saying, "Look, here are administrators that are going to convert our kids, they're going to impose sharia at public schools across the country," and all this crap. So that's my bigger fear. If there was an organization set up like that and if you were to start it even, I probably wouldn't join it. I'd be very concerned joining it, and that's no offense to you. I have a lot of respect for everything that you guys have done, even this study that you're doing.
>
> But I just don't want to be under the microscope. And I'm not saying that it would happen or not, but I don't even want to think about it. That's what I meant by I would feel like it would distract me from being a good administrator and best practices from being a good administrator, because then all of a sudden that every move I make, is it being scrutinized? And that's just too bad.

The role of political discourse and the media cannot be overlooked in a study of the lived experiences of American Muslim principals. It is important to understand the general perception of the political climate and media to contextualize the experiences of the participants that will be discussed in detail in the following chapters. Furthermore, it is crucial to reflect that an unhealthy political climate has the potential to create conditions that affect the school in its entirety.

All administrators, teachers, students, and the overall community can easily be impacted by such a climate, as it can lead certain individuals to feeling disadvantaged in their efforts to lead, teach, and learn. To ignore the impact of political climate ultimately undermines efforts of a school in its entirety.

While some may have not experienced severe hardships in their career as a result of their Muslim faith, some participants underwent traumatic experiences due to their religious identity, which impacted their psyche, spirituality, and overall health in many ways. The next chapter will discuss experiences of the participants that led them to feeling inferior and developing unconscious fear.

KEY CHAPTER IDEAS

- All 14 participants clearly indicated that political spectacle played a role in perpetuating political discourse and amplifying global events, and that the political climate played a pivotal role in the way that Islam and Muslims are portrayed.
- Additionally, all 14 participants drew attention to the 2016 presidential race in their interviews.
- The discussion on political climate also had a significant effect on the participants' psyche, leading them to develop serious fears and concerns.
- Participants acknowledged that the political climate has an effect on their leadership and how they interact with others.
- The word used most widely by the participants during the interviews was "media," which appeared 143 times throughout all transcripts and documents.
- All participants also indicated a lack of confidence in the U.S. media.

Chapter Six

Inferior and Foreign

Being Seen as the "Other" and Unconscious Fear

Since I'm a Muslim in a system that may [not] espouse tolerance, I just don't think I'm in a position to make mistakes like other people are.

INFERIOR AND FOREIGN: BEING SEEN AS THE "OTHER"

Jack Shaheen (2001) documented that the demonization of Arabs and Muslims stems back to 1896, when filmmakers first presented all Arabs and Muslims as enemies of Western civilization. The current political spectacle amplified by the media has led to the perception that Muslims are alien, foreign to the West, and not to be trusted. The participants in this study felt that political spectacle and the media coverage of Islam and Muslims portray negative perceptions of Muslims to their fellow Americans who have no personal or work interactions with American Muslims.

Eight of the participants, including both males and females, felt that they have to work twice as hard to show they are capable of their positions as principals. Six of the female participants felt they have to prove themselves three times as much because they are females in addition to being African American or of South Asian or Arab background and Muslim. Finally, the female participants who wear a hijab expressed even stronger sentiments than did the rest of the American Muslim principals.

Muslim women who are easily identifiable by their hijabs are often portrayed in the media as subjugated, uneducated, and oppressed as opposed to being educated or holding leadership positions (Aziz, 2012). One participant's teaching credentials were questioned by a parent due to her hijab. These assumptions and being treated as foreign or inferior weigh on many

American Muslim women, leading them to remove their hijabs or change their hijab style. Such an act, they believe, would draw less attention to themselves and better fit into American society. Three of the women in this study represent a portion of Muslim women who removed their hijabs, resorted to different scarf styles, or wore hats in the name of personal security.

According to the participants, this sense of inferiority and foreignness also affects their children, relatives, and friends as well as the American Muslim community as a whole. All participants were greatly concerned about the Muslim youth feeling vulnerable based on their being made to feel inferior and foreign in public spaces, such as in schools and on the Internet.

CAIR (2015) conducted a follow-up study in regard to the bullying of Muslim youth and found that 55% of nearly 500 American Muslim students reported that they were subjected to some form of bullying based on their religious identity. This is twice as high as the national statistic for students' reporting being bullied at school (CAIR, 2015).

More recently, a 2017 survey conducted by the Institute for Social Policy and Understanding (ISPU) found that 42% of Muslims with children in K–12 schools reported bullying of their children because of their faith (Mogahed & Chouhoud, 2017). The study also conveyed that teachers and school officials have participated in one in four bullying incidents involving Muslim students.

Feeling foreign and inferior was reported by the male participants who were perceived to be American Muslim based on their Muslim-sounding names, complexion, and having a beard. Among the females, one participant stated that in her school district, a fellow African American Muslim principal whose last name was Mohammad was told to change his name back to his Christian birth name to advance professionally. She herself has also experienced being treated as inferior and foreign. Irrespective of her racial background, she found herself on the no-fly list with thousands of Muslims, based on her name in the aftermath of 9/11. The no-fly list continues to contain the names of thousands of American Muslims of all ages.

In addition to American Muslims' being made to feel inferior and foreign on an individual basis, Muslim community projects are greeted with fear and suspicion. An example is the national trend of opposition to mosque purchases or expansions (Foley, 2010). Further, schools that offer Arabic, when seeking to expand their space, experience community opposition; One participant spoke of this in regard to his and a team of educators' attempt to purchase a larger building. This incident is reminiscent of the events surrounding the colocation of the Khalil Gibran International Academy in New York City in 2007.

Aziz believed that others' lack of education about or understanding of Islam and Muslims leads to serious misconceptions and results in Muslims' being made to feel foreign by their U.S. counterparts:

It's not as obvious, but there's still this perception and idea from what I gather that there's some mistrust. There's a misunderstanding of what a Muslim is. There's a misunderstanding of what Islam is. And there's very little education on what a Muslim is and what our way of life is and what we think, what we value. So there's still a lot of unknowns. There's still a lot of misconceptions.

African American Muslims in particular have come to recognize, that, in the aftermath of 9/11, their Muslim identity has added to whatever discrimination that they encountered as African Americans. This became a widespread sentiment among African American Muslims across the United States (Sides & Gross, 2015). Aziz noted that the Muslim diaspora had a rude awakening post-9/11. They experienced what it is like to be persecuted and came to empathize with the struggles of African Americans:

I think Muslims now understand what it means to be a Black American, to be persecuted, to be looked at in a particular way, to be prejudged, to be misunderstood. And I think that, yeah, some things have changed. But I think the overall tone, depending on where you are in the country, is still this idea that, you know, these Muslims, they could have three or four wives. They engage in supposedly subversive behavior. There's still some of that, some misnomers and still some issues related to us.

With the backdrop of political spectacle, the feeling of being inferior and of being foreign has become internalized for some participants. Aziz expressed his feelings about his ability to serve as a principal while being African American and Muslim:

I'm shocked that I'm a principal with the last name Mahmoud. I still can't believe it. Because I didn't think in the post-9/11 era that I would have the opportunity for academic upward mobility. I thought I would be pigeonholed. I thought I would be solely viewed on my last name. To this day, sometimes when people meet me, they say, "I expected an older gentleman, not looking like you." I don't even tell people I'm a principal. I tell them I'm a teacher because I don't even believe . . . my view and perception of the system is that I can be gone at any moment. So I don't even consider . . . I don't even share it with my childhood friends. I let them bring it up. I say, "I'm a teacher." That's the way I address anybody that I meet. And then whoever's with me may say differently, but I don't even profess it because this could be a fleeting moment in time. Anything can happen at any time. That's how I look at it. That's not a good way to look at things. But I'm realistic in terms of that.

I'm a black man. I'm a Muslim in America. That's a double-edged sword. So whatever way the sword swings, the head can go. Plus, any little mistake you make in this education system could be your last mistake. And human nature is to make mistakes.

Along with Aziz's disbelief that he is a principal in the post-9/11 era, there is also a conscious fear that his principalship could end at any moment due to his dual identity.

Aiman, who could be described as Aziz's counterpart, believed that if the day arrives that he can no longer be principal, he would not be upset by it. He replied that he would pack his bags and return to Pakistan. Aiman reflected on the impact of his foreign upbringing, which has influenced his views on U.S. nationalism and on raising his family in the United States:

> I think I owe a lot to the fact that I grew up in Pakistan and that I did not, just seeing White families, was not something to aspire to or something to feel less than about myself. I went to one of the best boarding schools in Asia, loved every moment of it. I don't have those things. . . . I did not grow up with fear or insecurity about who I was, and I was actually very, very . . . I am very, very grateful that I did not grow up in the United States. I have no intention of bringing my children up in this country, for fear that everyone that they'll see on TV, everyone that they'll see in a position of power, will be White, that their values would be different from ours. We very much intend for my parents and/or my wife's parents to live with us when we have kids, and that's not a model value that's very popular in the United States, and I don't want my kids to feel weird about it.
>
> I might be treated differently, of course. But I also feel very much like I'm living in a White man's country, right? I don't feel that this, as people who were born here or who grew up here, feel that this is their country. I don't feel that way. I'm the first to say that if I'm ever drafted for the military or something, I'm leaving. I don't believe in America's war. I don't believe that they [should] send girls and boys from poor shantytowns like the kinds I've seen in Texas to go fight for their freedom 20,000 miles away. I don't buy into any of this narrative, so, yeah, it's not my country, and I'm not going to ask for the rights that people who grew up here or live here are sure they must ask for to survive here. I'll just leave. It's a different way of . . . so while I do perceive racism, have perceived it maybe a few times, it has not bothered me. I felt very much like a guest in this country.

Even though Aiman views himself as a guest in the United States, he acknowledged his Western-centric education and expressed frustration at what he believes to be Americans' lack of knowledge of other cultures:

> Yeah, to me, as somebody who's traveled a lot internationally, and . . . I see that as a phobia in the American public of anything non-American, and currently the face of that phobia is Islam, unfortunately. People in this country, by and large, don't have a clue what goes on around the world. People are surprised, often surprised that I speak English as fluently as I do, and, yeah, so the ignorance of American people at large is frustrating and often irritating when it manifests itself in ways like, "How can you speak English so well?" If you pick any history book in the world, you'd know that where I come from, a part

of the world that was colonized by England for a very long time, and [I] have since had U.S.-centric education, also.

Rula, although of South Asian descent, identifies as a culturally American individual. Nevertheless, she acknowledged that others do not view her as such:

> It just felt like, at all times, like it felt like I always had to be more professional and more formal than a lot of my colleagues or my staff or other leaders or other administrators in the building because some people can joke about certain things, and, you know, they won't get in trouble, so to speak. They're not held up to that political correctness, but I was very well aware that if the smallest thing that I allude to or say sounds a little bit off, I will be held to a higher standard. I was always aware of that. And it is a cause of great stress, and you think about it a lot that, you know, this is unfair, you know. And I oftentimes like, you know, in my private moments I would sort of like compare and contrast that, oh, you know, my executive director or my assistant principal, if they had said this particular thing, no one would think twice about it. But if I had said that, I know for sure that a staff member or colleague would complain to the board of trustees about it.

With the backdrop of political spectacle, some participants also experienced prejudice and blatant discrimination. Najla discussed a harassment incident that she experienced with her husband in the months after 9/11:

> I recall going to a restaurant with my husband, and we were talking in English, but my husband also speaks Arabic, so I was going back and forth. I was talking English and then Arabic, English and then Arabic, and then I recall some man behind me saying, "You're in America; speak English," really loud for me to hear it. At first, I whispered to my husband. I said, "This is what the guy was saying," and he was like, "Just ignore him." Okay. So I kept on talking, but, intentionally, I raised my voice and spoke Arabic. He became a little bit more like, how do you say, like more animated? In spite of that, it's America: I can speak whatever language I want to speak. I can express my views the way I want to, so I said it a little louder, speaking Arabic and with a little more gusto, you know, loud. And I remember going out in the parking lot, and he came around in his car and did some circles around us while we were standing with his car. It was like screech, screech; that was scary.

Rula received similar sentiments from others, as seen in the following incident with a neighbor:

> We lived in a two-family house, so we had a neighbor upstairs. And I remember on the days following [9/11], she would make these bizarre comments like, "I respect everybody but I don't respect extremists. Are you extremist?" And I would just be like, "I've been living in the same building with you for the last, like, five years. Like, why is this even coming up?"

Rula reflected on the current climate for Muslims who live in the United States and shared her thoughts on being treated differently and the impact of suspicious treatment on young children:

> In terms of observation [of the state of Muslims in the United States], I think that things, at least on the surface, were stabilizing a little bit. And then the San Bernardino attacks had occurred, and the Paris attacks had occurred. And it sort of felt like the aftermath of 9/11 again. And in my current role as associate director of Youth Development, I have a portfolio of about 12 schools. So I go to different schools, and I remember going to a school, and the security guard knows me. And I was directed to the main office as soon as I walked in. And I was pretty annoyed. I said, "Why do I need to go to the main office? I come here all the time. You know me." And he was just like, "No. That's the policy."
>
> And I went to the main office, and, I mean, I had an attitude. I'm sorry. And I said to the secretary, I said, "Hello. I'm here for Child Center of New York. I come all the time. Why am I being directed to the main office?" And she was like, "All guests have to come into the main office." And I said, "No, they don't because I've come here about like eight times, and I just show my ID. And I walk in." And then she started catching an attitude with me, and then I just told myself to calm down, don't make waves. And I got my little sticker. I never needed a sticker before, and I went upstairs to the program office.
>
> I think it has changed in a way because I'm able to process it differently. So this is like, this is 13, 14 years later. And my concern now, and also in the community, I think it's with the kids. Like, how are the kids being impacted? What is the message? What is the narrative that they are going to be responsible for? Yeah. And especially now, I think, because my son is older. He's a teenager. He's 15 years old. That after all these recent events, how is he going to be treated? What questions is he going to be asked?

Although not all participants experienced discrimination, all experienced fear, either conscious or perhaps unconscious. Participants' reflections on their fears are presented in the next section.

UNCONSCIOUS FEAR

As noted from this study's analysis thus far, experiences of the participants may certainly potentially trigger unconscious fear. These fears range from losing their jobs to being targeted by parents, the school community, elected officials, or the media. The attitudes and behaviors of others toward Muslim school leaders has made American Muslim school leaders feel self-conscious and guarded about what they say and do for fear of being scrutinized and labeled extremist.

Some even expressed fear of being perceived as promoting "radical Islam" by performing simple religious tasks or talking about Islam. In this regard, many participants acknowledged a need to maintain political correctness to ensure their safety. In general, principals, as public figures, are guarded about what they say. However, Muslim principals exercise even more caution.

Eight of the participants shared that they were uncomfortable speaking about Islam to students, colleagues, and students' families even when students or staff brought up the topic. They also felt uncomfortable weighing in on global incidents that were perpetrated by people who call themselves Muslim, out of fear that they could say something that might come off as sympathetic or odd.

In instances in which they were made to discuss the incidents, participants kept the conversation to a minimum and changed the topic. Political correctness weighed heavily on all participants. Most participants felt that Muslim principals have to be cautious, on guard at all times, and think twice before speaking.

Aziz expressed his position on talking about Islam with members of his school community:

> No. [I'm] never comfortable. Never. Because that can be misconstrued as if I'm promoting Islam. I've been to a disciplinary hearing before because they thought I was promoting Islam. I don't like sharing any religious conversations or dialogues with my school community unless [it's with] a teacher in a historical class, and they're talking about religion. Outside of that, I don't speak on it. Even when students come to me and ask me questions, I ask, "What do your parents say? Interesting. Well, I defer." I'm not interested in talking about that because I don't want to get slapped on the wrist again.

Rula stated that she is always cautious about how her statements would be interpreted by staff, students, and parents. When asked whether she felt comfortable speaking about Islam, she responded:

> I rarely, if never, engage in discussions about Islam and with members of my school community. If I'm somehow looped into some discussion, I will openly say that I don't feel comfortable talking about my personal faith while performing my work role. When one speaks about faith, politics, etc., there has to be a level of mutual trust. I don't feel that trust in the work and school context. It's a highly charged world, and I refuse to be scapegoated into a corner.

Rula was extremely cautious about her speech and actions. She related an experience in which a number of Muslim students wanted to leave school premises on Fridays for prayer services. She made sure to follow the proper protocol and clarified the situation with the staff, as she did not want to be perceived as someone who was allowing students to leave the premises because they shared the same faith:

> I wanted to have that conversation with the staff because I did not want them
> to see it as, oh, we have a Muslim principal so she's just letting kids leave
> during lunchtime. And that was key because I wanted to set the precedent that,
> although I am Muslim, that I'm going to follow the proper protocol as per
> what New York State Education law indicates.

Unconscious fear and the need to maintain political correctness were constant themes throughout all of the participants' interviews, irrespective of conflicts that they may have experienced as principals. Participants believed that consequences for their actions would be much harsher because they are Muslim and did not believe that they would be pardoned for a mistake, as would their non-Muslim principal counterparts.

Najla discussed a moment when she was explaining to her school board about Muslim prayer times, as several students were requesting to leave their class to perform their prayer on time. Najla was informing them of the basics of the requirements, yet also realized that she was fearing that others may think she was promoting some sort of agenda:

> But I remember thinking; do they think that this is a new concern because now
> I'm sitting in this seat? Do you know what I mean? And I will say that the
> climate, what's happening now, this was the first time—for the first time, I felt
> like I hope they're not thinking that I'm now—it's a political agenda that I'm
> pushing. So I remember saying that. I remember clearly saying, "This is not a
> political agenda, or because I'm Muslim and they be non-Muslim." I said,
> "However, my number one fastest subgroup are Muslim, and this is a need.
> And I need to bring this to your attention that not only are we having calls
> from elementary principals, we're receiving phone calls from high school
> principals."

Najla relayed this experience as a moment of realization that Muslim principals need to remain extra conscious of what they say:

> It makes them think twice before they speak once. You know what I mean? I
> am really mindful of the words that come out of my mouth because it can be
> construed that I mean this or that. I mean I think yes, absolutely because
> there's a saying that you know, when you're given a lot of power, you're also
> expected—there's more expected from you, right? And I do believe being
> Muslim you have to think twice. You have to choose your words carefully.
> And I kind of think it's because of where we are now and the climate. Absolutely. It's unfortunate. It's unfortunate, but I think that every subgroup, every
> minority, every marginalized group has to go through this at one time.

Aziz dealt with incidents that resulted in his realization of the need to remain aware, fearful, and politically correct. He also explained that he found himself in situations that tested both his leadership and his faith. He had been called for a disciplinary hearing, having been charged with promoting Islam because he allowed students to attend a local mosque to perform their Friday prayers:

> I've been to a disciplinary hearing before because they thought I was promoting Islam. I got into trouble before . . . parents wrote me letters indicating that they want their children to attend a local mosque. I allowed them to go. I allowed students to have a particular area in the building where they could make prayers, and I received repercussions for that. Now, legally, they can have a room to pray. Legally, they can go to the mosque. But they said I was escorting them to the mosque. My argument was, okay, so even though I have the parents' consent to have them go to the mosque, I want to make sure they're safe and sound as they go.

Aziz recounted feeling a sense of violation and betrayal that someone in his school community would go so far as to call the superintendent's office:

> I have no idea [who made the complaints]. I guess it was some anonymous phone call. They came into the building one time. I let them sit in my office. And they were looking around. They saw a picture of a sister with a hijab on, saw another picture with a quote from the Quran. They told me I had to take that material down. And you know, I told them, "So you know, I do wear a kufi." And they acted like they didn't even understand what a kufi was. So I said, "A kufi is akin to wearing a yarmulke. So can I wear it?" I knew I could wear it. I just wanted to push the issue. And I told them, "I have my Quran on my desk. Is that an issue?" I know it wasn't an issue.

Weeks later, the investigation concluded with Aziz being informed that he could not walk students to the mosque or interact with the students from his school at the mosque, which left him feeling demoralized. A second investigation also occurred. This time it concerned Aziz being asked about accommodating Muslim teachers who wanted to leave the school building for Friday prayers:

> I got in trouble for that, too. Certain Muslim teachers were investigated. Teachers were investigated because they covered the classes for them. They were saying, "Well, it's a lack of instructional quality and time." I said, "It's only one period, one day, one week." I looked through the district's regulations, and it states, as long as it does not impede the instructional quality. So, yeah, I mean, I think three or four of us were under investigation because . . . within my building, going to the mosque, allowing children to pray . . . definitely can't make [prayer] with the children. You have to have them make prayer by themselves. You know, it's just . . . it's serious.
> There's actually four Muslim teachers, that one you would never know. It's a White sister. Now, you know, even when she converted and accepted, she wanted to do it as a secret because of reprisals and just because of what the perception is. That's how serious it is. . . . Whether it's still a secret or not is immaterial, so I just greet her now. . . . Yeah, it's very sad. But this system

does not promote or allow. I don't care what they say, for religious freedom. That's a nice word in the Constitution, but that's not the reality.

Aziz felt a sense of responsibility for his Muslim staff and his faith, even at the cost of losing his position to accommodate their religious freedom. He believed that as a result of these investigations, the district withheld a $10,000 bonus that Aziz earned for his students' earning high scores on standardized testing. When asked why he didn't inquire about the bonus, he stated that he would rather lose the money than put himself under the radar again.

Since these investigations, Aziz is cautious about the decisions that he makes that pertain to students and staff. He scrutinizes everything that comes across his desk, from staff-related activities to student social activities and trips. During the interview, the author witnessed Aziz questioning a teacher on the number of chaperones for a proposed trip, which was left out in the request submitted to him.

The teacher was short on chaperones and did not think there would be an issue, as he told Aziz that the students who were going were "mature." Aziz shot back at the teacher, stating, "You need to know the exact number of students and recruit chaperones to meet the 10 to 1 ratio. There are no cutting corners here. Remember, brother, my name is Aziz Mahmoud, and I am a Black Muslim man in America." Aziz was asked to expound on this interaction:

> I can't take chances in skirting the rules and regulations because I won't be afforded the opportunity of forgiveness, I don't think so. So I have to make sure everything is above board at all times. So if the ratio is 10 to 1, the ratio must be 10 to 1, and I can't take a chance of something taking place and then having it blow back on me because I think that the principal position is one of the most dangerous positions in the education system, period. And since I'm a Muslim, in a system that may [not] espouse tolerance, I just don't think I'm in a position to make mistakes like other people are.

As a result of these experiences, Aziz runs his school with great caution, always making sure everything is thoroughly and accurately done. He has an assistant principal who monitors students and who issues letters that pertain to staff's lateness, absences, punching in and out when leaving the school building to move a car, or even getting a cup a coffee from across the street. He and his assistant principals walk the halls to ensure that no classes are unattended by teachers and that instruction occurs at all times.

All disciplinary issues with students are processed by the letter of the law of the district and Aziz enforces them aggressively, which has created some tension between his staff and himself. His aggressive approach is a direct result of the unconscious fear that Aziz developed based on his traumatic experiences in the workplace.

Rula had also experienced conflict and distressing experiences in her role as principal, which led to the development of more serious fears. She became the principal of a charter school that was on the brink of closing, even though the status of the school turned around under her leadership and received an "A" rating for two consecutive years. Four years into her position, the school's newly elected board of trustees decided to hire an executive director to oversee the school. Rula and her director of operations colleague were informed by the board that they wanted to hire an executive director to be the "board's eyes and ears at the school level," which seemed peculiar to Rula.

Board members had expressed to Rula that they were hiring an executive director so that, "You're going to be freed up to focus more on instruction instead of worrying about the budget or worrying about suspensions or suspension hearings and things like that." The board had permitted Rula and the director of operations to interview candidates for the position; they interviewed three candidates. The school board of trustees had the final decision, and none of the candidates was awarded the position.

At the following board meeting, Rula and the director of operations were introduced to a newly hired executive director. Rula described her reaction as "speechless," as the executive director was not a candidate who had been interviewed by her or her colleague. Nevertheless, Rula complied with the decision and welcomed the executive director into the new position. Rula reflected back on the executive director's first week, recalling that the new hire had asked her whether she was a Muslim, to which Rula responded that she was. Rula noted that this was the first and only time that she had been asked about her religion by an employer.

Rula described her interactions with the executive director during the first week:

> She came in, and she wanted to have like a little . . . I guess, a meet and greet during the school day when she first came in. And she first explained to me that her brother, a fireman, was killed in 9/11. And I expressed my condolences, and I said, "You know, at my mosque, there was a young man who was an EMS worker and he's known to my family. And he was also killed in 9/11." And then she said, "Oh, you're Muslim?" And I said, "Yes, I am a Muslim." And then she asked me, "Is your husband a Muslim?" And I said, "Yes, he is." And she said, "Oh, was he born a Muslim?" And I was like, "No. No." I was like, "He embraced Islam in college." And she's like, "Oh. Oh. How old was he?" And she was very interested in that. And she asked me, do I practice Islam and things like that. So I felt that it was a little bit strange. But, of course, I didn't want to question it. So I let it be.

The executive director went out of legal bounds with her inquiries about Rula and her family's religious background. One can surmise that she was motivated by political spectacle, which for her, was very close to home, with the loss of her brother on 9/11. Rula then shared another encounter that made her very uneasy but feared expressing her professional concern because she was afraid that her feedback would be seen as anti-American and as espousing Islamic extremist views, as these were the perceptions that many non-Muslims had of Muslims. Rula recounted:

> The following week during our cabinet meeting, she had asked, "What does the school do for 9/11?" And I said, "We have a moment of silence. We recognize 9/11 on the public address that we have for the kids. And then we have a moment of silence." And then she said, "That's not good enough." And she then launched into, like a, I think it was, like, a 10-point bullet plan of, like, what we need to do for 9/11, and why don't we commemorate it in a respectful fashion? And people died for us in 9/11. And I was, like, whoa, and it just got weirder from there, got weirder. She wanted each teacher to come up with a lesson plan regarding 9/11 at some point during the day. And it was pretty much, pretty much strange to me because we already had, like, during advisory and during the PA, recognition of it. . . . But I couldn't object because she was my supervisor. And yeah, so we did that.

Rula recalled a number of other incidents that made her feel uneasy:

> [I]ncidents, both micro and macro aggressions, started to tally up. And just in case, the person in my head said, the little Rula in my head said, you need to keep a log of all this stuff because something about this isn't right. And I kept a log of the moments where I felt harassed or just felt weird or weird questions or things like that.

In January of that school year, Rula's supervisor brought to school 9/11 commemoration T-shirts with her brother's picture on it to give out to select staff and an administrator. Rula retold that moment where she saw herself as the symbolic enemy:

> [S]he gave it to the other administrator, but she didn't give it to me. And I felt that that was really weird. She gave it to two of the teachers that she liked, the guidance counselors, things like that. And she was standing right in front of me while she was giving it to people. And then she called the other administrator, and she gave it to her. And I was standing right there, and I thought when is she going to give it to me? Like I'm the principal of the school, you know? And she didn't give it to me. And she looked at me while she was giving it to people. And it just seemed to me like so high school, like so, like, pathetic. And I was like, wow, because she did not want me wearing a T-shirt with her brother's name on it.

Rula experienced blatant and subtle discriminatory actions and remarks that pertained to her faith. She was made to feel like the outsider by the executive director and a staff member whom she hired:

> I remember she [the new hire] was very warm when she came onboard. And then, suddenly, she just stopped talking to me. And then, they would always have their little chats in the office. They would always be together during lunch. During Twin Day, they were twins together. She was the same [ethnicity] as the executive director, Italian. But they would talk . . . at length about how both their moms would be in the kitchen making sauce and sausages. And, oh, "You don't eat meat, Rula." "No, I don't eat meat; vegetarian." Yeah. And then, she started bringing in this woman to, like, little conferences that she had, no, like, you know, in-house cabinet meeting conferences, meetings with parents, things like that that she really did not belong at, but she would be there.

Rula began to feel that the executive director was grooming the new hire for a higher position, possibly that of Rula's. Rula hoped that despite what she was experiencing, she was not going to be let go because she was Muslim. She convinced herself that it would happen only if she were ineffective as principal. Rula shared her thought process:

> I wanted to think that [it was because I was Muslim], but I kept on pushing it away because if I was going to be let go, I wanted to be let go or pushed out, or however you want to phrase it, for something valid. And I remember every day, ever since I was a teacher, even before I left for the day, I wanted to call every parent that I needed to call, speak with every kid that I wanted to speak to, speak with every teacher, and straighten everything out on my desk. So if I was going to, quote, unquote, be removed from my position, I wanted to be removed for something substantial that I did. My school was failing. My kids were not achieving . . . something [like that].

Rula's concerns ultimately became a self-fulfilling prophecy. The executive director realized that Rula took pride in her work and started to attack Rula's performance as a principal. Rula recalled the executive director reprimanding her in front of a new teacher:

> [A] teacher came in and said her kids did really well in math. We were going to have a pizza party, and I said, "A pizza party is a great idea." I said, "Please make sure to send consent forms to the parents to let them know that, instead of having the regular school day lunch, the kids will be eating pizza party lunch. Please let them know that the pizza that will be ordered will have dairy in it in case kids are lactose intolerant." And she flipped out. "Why you such a micro manager? Why do we need to send consent forms home," blah, blah, blah, blah, blah. And she berated me in front of the teacher. And I said to her, "According to New Jersey School System, you know, and also as a measure in which we are collaborating with the parents, we want to inform them, No. 1,

that we're having this beautiful prize given to their kids. That's good publicity. No. 2, we're letting them know that if their dietary requirements don't align with what we're serving, they can opt out." She's like, "That's just bullshit." The teacher was a first-year teacher, very young. She stood there silently. She was struck mute. And then when I saw her in the hallway later, she said, "Ms. Big, I'm sorry if I got you in trouble." And I said to her, she didn't get me in trouble. I'm like, "It's okay."

The executive director chiseled away at Rula's authority as principal. Rula recounted how the executive director hounded her to apply for professional development:

So she was like, "You need to do PDs [professional development hours]. You need to do PDs." And I was like, "Frankly, like, right now, I'm not interested in doing PDs. I'm interested in stabilizing the school." Because this was the year after the network had dissolved. And our charter was under renewal. And I wanted to be there 24/7. And I said, "Okay. I'll do a PD." So I applied to Harvard, and I got accepted into their Principal Leadership Program. When I got accepted into the program, she said to me, "You need to show your staff that you're engaged in PDs." And I said, "So do you want me to tell them that I was accepted to Harvard?" "Yeah, tell them that. Tell them." Like that's how she was. And I was like, "Okay." So during the PD, I got up and I said, "I'm getting up now to tell them." And she's like, "Okay." And so then I got up and I said, "You know, I have some really good news. I was accepted to," blah, blah, blah. And they all gave me an ovation. She got up, screamed at the top of her lungs, at the top of her lungs. I had 50 witnesses in front of me. "You can't say that. You can't say that."

Rula had been set up for public humiliation in front of her staff. The staff as a whole witnessed for themselves how Rula was being treated. When Rula sought them out to come to her defense when speaking with the board of trustees, however, they were afraid for their own jobs. Rula explained:

No one would believe me. No one would believe me. You know what I'm saying? It's like, it's like a made-for-TV movie. And so then I pulled a couple of people aside after it, and I said, "You just saw what happened." "We didn't see anything." They were scared.

A week later, the executive director called Rula into her office to inquire about the missed state education deadline for the school's student enrollment data. Rula recounted the interaction:

"Why didn't the BEDS [Basic Educational Data System] data go in?" Because that's how she spoke to me. And I said, "The BEDS data did go in. I did all the teacher surveys." She's like, "No, the other demographic stuff."

Rula explained that she did not know about the need to enter the additional school data into the district's system, as all state education communications were transferred to the executive director upon her request when she started:

> I'm like, "Because if you did [get the email], you could have reminded me." And she said, "It's not about that. It's about the fact that you have no leadership capacity whatsoever." And I had to sit down because, for me, my integrity at work is paramount to me. Because I take leadership very seriously, and it's also because [of] public funding. I'm a public employee, and I want to serve with honesty, integrity, and compliance.

Rula recalled that she was so shaken up by this exchange that the executive director said:

> "You need to calm [down]. . . . You need to calm yourself down and get a hold of yourself. And the way that you're behaving now is not how a leader behaves. And you're not a leader." And so I started crying and I started shaking. And I said to her, "The only way we can work together is if we have trust. And the tone that you're speaking to me right now in says you don't trust me." And she says, "That's right. I don't trust you." And so, at that point I had to excuse myself because I felt like I was going to have a breakdown.

Rula went back to her office and, moments later, had a seizure for the first time. An ambulance was called to the school, and Rula was taken to the hospital and admitted into the emergency room. Rula was told that she suffered from a seizure due to her stressful work environment. While in the hospital, not a single board member called to check on her. Weeks later, Rula wrote the board of trustees a 10-page letter about what she experienced at the hands of the executive director.

She did not get a response to the letter but did receive an email shortly after that informed her that the board was not renewing her contract. In addition, the board called Harvard to withdraw Rula from the program because they had agreed to pay for her. Rula was able to convince Harvard to allow her to pay for the program so that she could attend.

To this day, Rula suffers from anxiety as a result of her work experience. When asked whether she would ever file a lawsuit, Rula emphasized that the entire experience took a toll on her health and well-being and that she has no intention of revisiting the trauma. She is currently still seeking treatment for her anxiety and seizures and is undergoing therapy.

As seen in the case of Rula, challenges in the workplace also can lead to internal issues. The participants mentioned in this chapter have displayed trends of developing unconscious fears and the need to maintain political correctness. In some cases, their experiences led to growing traumatic perceptions that ultimately affected their own well-being. As the next chapter will exhibit, these fear and experiences resulted in a change in spirituality for some participants, namely, a decrease in spirituality level or lessening in their practice of the faith.

KEY CHAPTER FINDINGS

- Eight of the participants, including both males and females, felt that they have to work twice as hard to show they are capable of their positions as principals.
- Six of the female participants felt they have to prove themselves three times as much because they are females in addition to being African American or of South Asian or Arab background and Muslim.
- All participants were greatly concerned about the Muslim youth feeling vulnerable based on their being made to feel inferior and foreign in public spaces, such as in schools and on the Internet.
- In addition to American Muslims' being made to feel inferior and foreign on an individual basis, Muslim community projects are greeted with fear and suspicion.
- Experiences of the participants may certainly potentially trigger unconscious fear. These fears range from losing their jobs to being targeted by parents, the school community, elected officials, or the media.
- The attitudes and behaviors of others toward Muslim school leaders has made American Muslim school leaders feel self-conscious and guarded about what they say and do for fear of being scrutinized and labeled extremist.
- Eight of the participants shared that they were uncomfortable speaking about Islam to students, colleagues, and students' families even when students or staff brought up the topic.
- The need to maintain political correctness was also a prevalent trend in this study.
- The stress of inferiority also led to traumatic psychological results for some participants, as was the case with Rula.

Chapter Seven

Spirituality

The only relief that I had, the only thing that kept me sane was prayer.

The thought of spirituality in the context of public education raises the common belief to maintain distance in spirituality, keeping in mind the separation of church and state clause. However, there has been research that states spirituality complements and enhances school leadership. According to Robertson (2008), a school leader must be sincere and able to look beyond the mundane managerial responsibilities of the job to personalize the nature of his or her work. This *head-and-heart* approach to leadership invokes a spiritual dimension.

The connection between spiritual leadership and educational leadership is solidified as one begins to reorient his or her leadership as a deeply personal experience for oneself. Robertson argues that the traits emblematic of a spiritual leader, including compassion, integrity, and perseverance, are not exclusive to spiritual or religious professions but can be cultivated only when a spiritual or deeply personal connection is forged.

In this study, spirituality is displayed through two aspects: being spiritually connected to a higher being at all times through the embracement of the philosophy "Islam is a way of life," and physical worship, which consists of praying five times a day, fasting during Ramadan, making hajj (pilgrimage to Mecca), almsgiving, and, for women, the wearing of the hijab. All participants declared Islam as a way of life in word and deed. Eight of the 14 participants indicated that spirituality enhanced their leadership.

EFFECTS OF SPIRITUALITY

Although a greater portion noted that their spirituality was not affected by their leadership role, their responses indicated otherwise. Specifically, their position as a school leader in a climate fueled by political spectacle hindered their spirituality in the following three areas: not performing their daily prayers, not attending obligatory Friday (Jummah) prayers, and women not wearing the hijab.

PRAYER

When participants were asked to voluntarily share whether they were able to make their prayer during work hours, seven of the 14 felt comfortable responding to the question. The other seven felt that it was too personal to share. Some participants shared that they pray in their offices without staff members knowing due to the fear of their intentions being misconstrued.

When Aiman was asked about prayer, he shared his current practice and then significant reflections on the reason for his abandoning prayers. He referred to his stepmother's experience of conversion to explain his belief that Muslims, not the religion of Islam, drove him away from practicing the faith:

> When I used to live in the United States, I used to fast all the time and pray five times a day. I started distancing myself from my spirituality when I moved back to Pakistan. The attack on my spirituality, unfortunately, has not come from living in the West; it has come very much from living amongst Muslims who have just been, yeah, just not done a really good job of living up to the aspirations of the faith. My stepmother, the convert, she's White, and she's from Spain. I really like and respect her . . . she didn't convert to marry my father; she converted six years before they ever met. She's from Spain, and she was in Barcelona at the time. She said something to me that I think about a lot. She said, "I was undeniably in love with Islam before I started living amongst Muslims," because she was in Spain and then was in Colombia, where she converted while doing her thesis as a very, very devout Catholic . . . doing her thesis on the personification of Christ in different religions and really found the story in Islam to be the one that made the most sense to her.
>
> So it's unfortunate, but the actions of a lot of Muslims, particularly after 9/11, have left me just a little disappointed, to where I find it hard to align, especially spiritually, with the Muslim faith.

Aiman's position stems from his being out of touch with the local Muslim community and his disengagement from Muslim affairs in the United States. It could be argued that Aiman's perspective is a result of his viewing the Muslim community from a lens colored by political spectacle.

Najla stated that she did not engage in all her obligatory prayers due to the demands of her professional life. Nevertheless, she acknowledged that prayer was her primary source of relief and inner peace:

> No. I don't pray five times a day. I've had these spurts of when I pray all the time. I think, once I start focusing on my religion and my spirituality and my faith, I feel I would give it some thought, but it's been really busy in my professional [life], and I've always struggled with this, the balance in my professional and my personal life. As a principal, the pressure, especially now with the new reform agenda and turning around the school, you have the eyes of the district leaders on you, the state leaders. You have parents on you. You have teachers expecting you to be balanced. Like, give us pressure but also support, but don't push us too hard. You have your family. It was too much, and the only relief that I had, the only thing that kept me sane was prayer. So I didn't pray five times a day, but the only thing that gave me relief was prayer.

FRIDAY OBLIGATORY PRAYER

Another spiritual component that was discussed by participants was Jummah, the Friday prayer, a weekly service that men are obligated to attend. Women are excused from the obligation but are encouraged and allowed to attend. The men who did not attend Jummah prayer at a mosque reasoned that they did not feel comfortable leaving the school out of fear of emergency. As one participant stated:

> It's almost like you're in a situation, one that's not right, but you have to protect yourself. Because if I left because I had a meeting with a superinten- dent, that's one thing, but if I left to go to the Mosque, then that becomes a whole other story in the newspaper. And it's sad. But if I leave, and the principal's at Mosque, wow, two kids were shot through the window, that story just ends up becoming [about the Muslim principal, not the two students who were shot]; people add to it, you know. So I really, I'm always thinking, forward-thinking and thinking ahead and thinking about not even really pro- tecting me but protecting my children. And it's sad that we have to think that way in this world, but it's the harsh reality.

Other participants had also expressed that they did not feel comfortable to request religious accommodations for the Friday prayer. However, some have come to somewhat a spiritual resolve by finding ways such as one of the participants who Livestreams the service from his local mosque in his office. Living in a climate consumed by political spectacle perpetuates individuals infringing on their very own rights as is the case with some participants in this study.

In contrast, Aziz attends the Friday prayer and weekly informs his super-intendent, thus fulfilling a spiritual practice and obligatory component of his faith:

> I go to prayer services. I still email the superintendent [about this], period, all the time, even though we already had this discussion. But you have to tell your superintendent where you are at all times. If not, that's abandonment of duty. And you will, you will pay a price for that.

ARTICLES OF FAITH

In regard to wearing a hijab, all eight female participants had donned a hijab at some point in their life. A hijab, as noted previously, is a cloth that is designed to cover the female's hair and is a form of Islamic spiritual practice. The purpose of such a practice is meant to remind the individual that her main submission should be to God before all worldly matters. It additionally represents a form of modesty, where emphasis is to be directed toward one's character and intellect rather than physical attraction. This spiritual practice was heavily affected in three participants. Two participants made a conscious decision to no longer wear a hijab in the workplace, and another changed the style of her hijab as a safety concern.

Prior to 9/11, Najla taught while wearing a hijab and continued to do so after 9/11, until she decided to advance in educational leadership in 2005. She came to the conclusion that wearing a hijab would be a hindrance to her leadership. This sentiment was shared by her family and friends and thus, Najla removed her hijab when she started the leadership program. Najla recounted her thought process about her leadership role as affected by her wearing a hijab:

> Will people listen to me? Will they connect with me? Because I'm thinking that leadership is about connecting. When you think about leadership . . . initially I was very fragile and I thought about being popular . . . so will I have people that will like me?

Najla discussed how she came to believe that wearing a hijab would not affect her leadership:

> I have always had a love/hate relationship with the hijab. I always felt strong, confident and purposeful when I wore the hijab. As a teacher, my students embraced me. Unfortunately, the people closest to me made me feel self-conscious. So, while I was a student studying to become a school leader I took off the hijab. In 2007, when I first began my career as a school administrator, I did believe that the hijab would have a negative impact on my leadership style. I felt that the hijab would distract my staff from "listening" to what I have to

say. . . . I am proud being Muslim, but as a young leader, I did not know how it would impact my leadership, and so I chose not to wear it. . . . I remember telling myself, Will I have people that will like me and listen to me, or will this, the hijab, put something into their mind, their mental model or trigger, something that they won't even listen? I know now that it's not about what you look like but what you stand for: your core values, how you inspire people. I think if I went in wearing a paper bag, I know that, based on my experience, that my teachers would follow me and that I would have the support of all the families.

Upon completing the program, she became a principal and continued to have the same reservations about exhibiting her faith via the hijab. Najla struggled internally with her decision. Although she wanted to succeed in her new leadership capacity, she also wanted to remain true to her faith. Najla's spiritual struggle in regard to wearing a hijab continued, but her faith in God remained intact and she found herself reaching to him daily for sustenance.

Najla currently is working at the district level, where she faces new challenges concerning her faith. The Muslim student population in a few of the schools is requesting a space to pray, and Najla has become the go-to individual on issues that pertain to the Muslim community. She is concerned that, although she seeks to remain sincere to her faith, she does not want to be seen as pursuing a personal political agenda. In regard to the hijab, Najla believes that one day she will return to wearing the hijab and feel the sense of pride and confidence that she once had.

Other female participants provided different reasoning for their removal of the hijab. One participant explained that she only removes her hijab during work hours, while donning it outside of her workplace. She believes that the hijab would lead to mistrust from the school community. This also is an instance of the tension between professionalism and spirituality, as removing the hijab during certain hours conflicts with the spiritual practice of wearing it at all times in public. One participant stated that she continues to wear the hijab; however, she has changed her style of wearing it to conform more to social cultural norms.

THE ROLE OF FAITH

Participants also were asked to reply, on a scale of 1–10, in regard to how heavily faith plays a role in alleviating the everyday stress and pressures as a principal. Of the 14 participants, seven answered 10, two answered 8, two answered 7, one answered 6, one answered 5, and one answered 3, with a mean score of a little over 8. Najla personally chose to describe her role of faith at 8. Aziz, who chose to describe the role of faith in his professional life as a 10, explained: "Yes, in a sense that it relieves my stress, it relieves the pressure that I may be going through. When I make *salat* [prayer], it helps me every single day."

Aiman, who appeared to distance himself from Islam and Muslims throughout his interviews, used a rating of 7. He did not offer much of an explanation, thus the author reminded him of the sentiments that he shared in his first interview, in which he was asked, "Do you feel that certain aspects of Islam, which you genuinely espouse to and are very connected to, are an inspiration for you to be the best leader you could be in your job?" Aiman was asked whether his primary response would suffice for an explanation of his rating. He had answered, "Yes," and presented his initial thoughts on spirituality:

> The same aspects of Islam that still, I feel very connected to, as I say, to make me want to be the best leader that I can be, to make me want to prioritize the job that I have, the work that I do, over sort of material things, it makes me want to be the best son that I can be. You know, when I was 20 years old and driving a sports car and was dating a beautiful girl, my mother was a divorcee and living in Pakistan at the time, and her brother was moving to Saudi Arabia, he was a doctor, to run a hospital there, and she was going to have to live by herself for the first time, which felt very strange. I left my life here, at that time really enjoying it because I was in college, an undergrad, to go live with her, and I think that's part of my Islamic upbringing.
>
> I was a dropout for seven years, but went back to live with her, and that's a part of being a Muslim. It was very clear to me that my priority was to live with that, and I think that that comes from being a Muslim, having grown up as a Muslim and also having grown up around Muslims.
>
> Everything since has happened for the better, and I think that, when you continue to keep making choices based on sort of knowing that a higher power is watching and wants you to do the right things, that comes very much from having the faith that I do and that Allah is watching, and as long as I'm honest to him and as long as I'm honest to myself, everything else will take care of itself. I approach the world that I do have to make some very, very difficult decisions as, you know, being a principal. And I always ask myself that sort of, "What would God want me to do? What would I want for my own kids, if and when I have them?" That's what I'm going to do. And so far, I mean, it's just been a few months, but so far there haven't been any major screw-ups.

Rula, reflecting on her own experiences, chose to rate the role of faith in handling her everyday pressures of work with a 5.5. She offered a fascinating reflection that one may always be challenged in life, but that is what will inevitably happen when you are trying to make a positive change in life:

> I felt throughout my years in education I've always been aligned with like social justice and like my heroes, like Malcolm X, Maya Angelou, Angela Davis, Zora Neale Hurston, Spike Lee even, you know, I've always had this sense of social justice. So I know that above all of it, above all spirituality,

above all positive disposition, all of this is this sense that like if you strive to do good and if you strive to make a positive change, you're always gonna come across some type of challenge. So in my mind, the way that I framed it is that I've been challenged my entire life. And whether it's because I'm a woman of color, I'm a Muslim, or whatever it is, an immigrant, I'm gonna come across some challenge. And I always used to joke with my friends that nothing ever comes easy for Rula and so it's yet another challenge. And other people face far more profound challenges.

Spirituality has the potential to be affected by one's job demands, as seen in some of the participants' responses. Sometimes, however, spirituality can enhance their leadership. As a result of their spiritual connection, some participants felt the need to personally engage with non-Muslims to break down the Islamophobic frames of political spectacle, which shapes how most people view Muslims.

As this chapter exhibited, participants' spirituality had been significantly affected by their experiences as a school principal. In many cases, there had been negative effects on the individual leading to missing the performance of the obligatory prayers, absence at the Jummah prayer, and the removal of the hijab. However, there were also positive spiritual perspectives stemming from their experiences, which in turn results in communication and engagement with others. And through this act, participants were able to break down the Islamophobic frames of political spectacle that have shaped the way most people view American Muslims post-9/11, as discussed in the next chapter.

KEY CHAPTER FINDINGS

- Eight of the 14 participants indicated that spirituality enhanced their leadership.
- Although a greater portion noted that their spirituality was not affected by their leadership role, their responses indicated otherwise.
- When participants were asked to voluntarily share whether they were able to make their prayer during work hours, seven of the 14 felt comfortable responding to the question. The other seven felt that it was too personal to share.
- The men who did not attend Jummah prayer at a mosque reasoned that they did not feel comfortable leaving the school out of fear of emergency.
- In regard to wearing a hijab, all eight female participants had donned a hijab at some point in their life. Two participants made a conscious decision to no longer wear a hijab in the workplace, and another changed the style of her hijab as a safety concern.
- Responses overall indicated that spirituality can be affected by one's job demands; however, at times it can also enhance their leadership abilities.

Chapter Eight

Education and Communication Over Political Spectacle and Additional Findings

Collective guilt has left Muslim individuals mentally exhausted.

EDUCATION AND COMMUNICATION OVER SPECTACLE

Living and working in a post-9/11 world against the backdrop of political spectacle has its challenges for American Muslim principals. There are times, however, when human interactions can break through the political spectacle. All participants discussed serendipitous dialogues with non-Muslim individuals that left these individuals with a positive impression of Muslims.

Spiritually, Muslims are obligated to build bridges between themselves and other communities, as drawn from a verse in the "Dwellings" chapter in the Quran: "Oh mankind, indeed we have created you from a male and female and made you peoples and tribes so that you may know one another" (49:13). Inspired by this calling, American Muslims welcome opportunities to personally engage with non-Muslims as a part of their faith. Through this act, participants were able to break down the Islamophobic frames of political spectacle, which have shaped the way most people view American Muslims post-9/11.

One participant, Rana, shared her interaction with the woman who was enamored by her wind-blowing hijab, that Rana referred to as the "flag of Islam." The woman saw an image of the hijab that was out of the context of what is typically presented about Muslim women in the media. She saw a woman enjoying the boat ride with her family and appeared at peace and carefree. The colors of Rana's hijab were flowing like a sailboat in the distance. This image intrigued her to approach Rana. Their short exchange took this woman to a place where she had not expected go, to learn about Islam and Muslim women.

Another participant, Lana, described a "humanizing" experience at a state education conference. She felt that, initially, she was being judged due to her wearing a hijab while offering a presentation on education policy. When she presented her speech and later interacted with session participants, it became clear to her that she had defied the stereotype of the uneducated submissive Muslim woman in the minds of the session participants. Lana described feeling that the tension in the room was dissipating, instead feeling camaraderie between her education colleagues and herself; one even asked whether he could bring members of his district to visit her school.

Najla shared an incident in which the city teacher's union representative visited her school regarding a grievance concerning Najla filed by the teachers and recounted:

> I remember crying, and I said to her, "You know, I just know that Allah is going to take care of me." We talked about faith, and [she asked], "Do you believe in God?" I was like, "Yeah, absolutely." That's when I opened up about Islam and who I am. She said that, "What we learn is that we turn to God in our time of need, and this is going to be okay. You have to remember how God loves and how we have to believe that people are good." So we had this really deep conversation about Islam and Christianity and how they overlap and how with both of them it comes down to people first, loving people first, and how compassion moved the way people thought and everything through talking and being nice. And so we shared our different backgrounds but how we have similarities and how, in her case, Jesus led his people and how Mohammad led his people. So that was beautiful. For me, it was an introduction to a really deep relationship, a lasting relationship between Jamie and I that, even now, she comes to me, and we just have these really deep conversations about stuff.

Najla essentially humanized Islam and Muslims in this instance and described this interaction as a bond that changed their relationship. She also recounted a televised interview in regard to the FBI's arrest of a Muslim. The non-Muslim man who was interviewed about Muslims explained that he had grown up with Muslims and found them to be kind, loving people, thus humanizing Muslims to the public:

> Most recently, the FBI made an arrest of an ISIS suspect, and a news reporter asked a young non-Muslim, non-Arab man if he was fearful of his neighbors who are Muslims. He stated, "No. I know them. I grew up with them. They are kind, loving people." The reporter asked, "Do you think the neighborhood's reaction will be similar to 9/11?" He said, "The neighborhood didn't react negatively in 2001 because we know that Islam doesn't promote violence. . . .

> People in other communities reacted the way they did because they were
> fearful because they don't know Islam or Muslims like we do."

The mentioning of education and communication over spectacle was also prevalent throughout Aiman's interviews when discussing his experience and the school climate he inherited at his school. His school embraces a philosophy of tolerance and acceptance of all people, including him and other Muslim students. This stems from genuine dialogue and reflection on how to create an environment that values and celebrates diversity.

The hope is that these forms of exchange will further inspire non-Muslims to inquire about Islam and Muslims as well as see beyond political spectacle and interrupt Islamophobic frames based on interactions with American Muslims. Ultimately, while themes such as political spectacle are prevalent in society, it would be of greater benefit for minorities to first seek others as allies as opposed to holding the belief that "others" are holding purely negative perceptions.

ADDITIONAL FINDINGS

Throughout the research process, two specific noteworthy findings emerged: collective guilt and social responsibility. The notion of collective guilt was found in a study by Hilal (2014). Hilal examined the war on terror in terms of how it has been framed and the actors involved in the construction of the Muslim image, with a focus on the ways in which Muslims have been demonized and positioned as collectively responsible for acts of terrorism.

The theme of collective guilt, which Hilal terms "collective responsibility," was found among 72% of her participants, who saw it as an issue that American Muslims face. She noted that her participants stated that an act of terrorism initiated by a non-Muslim is simply an individual act, "whereas an act perpetrated by a Muslim is a collective act worthy of intensified scrutiny." Related to Hilal's (2014) findings, seven participants believe that an unfair burden has been placed on American Muslims because it was only a small fringe minority who were responsible for the terrorist attacks. Many American Muslims feel offended when people ask them to apologize for or condemn terrorism when they also were vulnerable to being victims of terrorism (Mastracci, 2015).

Collective guilt has caused American Muslims to stifle their voices and to be further marginalized. One of the female participants expressed her frustration on the notion of collective guilt:

> So it kind of alters your perspective and, also, something that you always have
> to feel that you have to disassociate yourself: "I'm not that type of Muslim.
> Those are not Muslims, these are so-called Muslims." And you feel like you're

always on the defensive. You have to defend or show the world. I mean, for God's sake, what if I cut off a driver while I'm driving, because, you know, it happens. The first thing, my initial reaction is to go back, because I don't want them to see that I wear the hijab because I represent Islam. So these are the things that constantly come into play because you always feel you don't want to give another bad rap. Even though it's not as extreme, but it's just this constant feeling of guilt, but you're not a part of that guilt.

Aiman also expressed this form of collective guilt:

I don't think that the issues . . . we are over a billion Muslims in the world, so to be represented globally by 20,000 who have made choices to go and blow up places and kill people seems quite ridiculous to me. Collective guilt has left [Muslim] individuals mentally exhausted.

Aziz explained the burden of Muslims needed to prove that they do not fit the stereotypes that others impose on them:

So unfortunately, we have a burden and the burden is to prove this misnomer wrong, to prove the stereotypical image wrong. So we carry around with us a lot of weight on our shoulders where it relates to how we conduct ourselves, what we say, how we deal with certain situations. It's . . . the situation is much bigger than us. So we represent something that even though we may not want to represent it, we do. So we have to be above reproach at all times, or be looped into that stereotype. So a lot of what we do, we try to break the stereotypes.

The second additional finding was the notion of social responsibility. Most of the participants expressed the need for American Muslims to be more civically engaged by serving underrepresented students and volunteering in their communities. Civic engagement historically has been the key to every minority community's becoming part of the fabric of the U.S. community. This has proven to be the case for the Jewish and Catholic communities as well upon their arrival in the United States (Weiner, 2006).

As school leaders, the participants felt a need to protect students through condemning all forms of stereotypes, discrimination, racism, and bigotry. They also felt a sense of social responsibility to civically and politically engage their communities locally and nationally. Rula, as mentioned in the previous chapter, contextualized her passion for social justice in terms of her spirituality, which she viewed as a catalyst for achieving justice and seeking the best for all. As she had explained:

I felt that this act of having faith or spirituality ultimately becomes a political act, you know, in a greater context. And so, you know, it's also, it's directly connected [to] you as a person of faith, wanting the best for everybody who is around you. So it lends itself to justice, to fair play.

The national catalyst for American Muslim civic engagement was the Chapel Hill murders of Razan Mohammad Abu-Salha and Yusor Mohammad Abu-Salha and her husband, Deah Barakat. Their murders shocked the nation and shook the American Muslim community. These three young people had dedicated their short lives to serving their fellow man out of a love for their country. American Muslim communities across the United States engaged in a national food collection campaign called "Feed Their Legacy" to memorialize their lives, donating the food to local food banks and pantries. Within one year, there were 287 food drives that collected 172,612 cans of food (Feed Their Legacy, 2015).

The experiences of the participants had led to recognizing the responsibility of creating some sort of forum or Muslim principal group composed of other principals who share similar challenges or experiences. Such an endeavor would provide others with networking opportunities, the sharing of ideas, and most importantly, support. While many encouraged the notion of creating a group catered toward Muslim principals in public schools, there were also some who expressed that they would greater benefit in a gathering that is meant for all minority groups:

> Rather than isolating Islam and Islamic principles and thinking, right now we need to push more into the mainstream so that we're not seen as something different or in opposition to American Society, but more of an integral part of it. There would be a lot to offer. For example, when you go to Islamic conferences, sometimes you only see Muslims and everything is from an Islamic perspective. But how do you then take that and then go back into the larger society in which we all work and operate? There doesn't seem to be that crossover back into being able to take that and use it.

The analysis of the six themes of political climate, role of the media, inferior and foreign: being seen as the "Other," unconscious fear, spirituality, and education and communication over spectacle, as well as the two additional findings of collective guilt and social responsibility, has provided an in-depth understanding of American Muslim principals of public schools. This analysis is used, in the next chapter, to address the research questions.

KEY CHAPTER FINDINGS

- Personal interactions and communication have often led to greater understanding between the participants and their school community members.
- To humanize the "Other" seems to be an effective method in building bridges, according to some participants.
- The theme of collective guilt was found among 72% of Hilal's (2014) participants, who saw it as an issue that American Muslims face.

- Most of the participants of this study expressed the need for American Muslims to be more civically engaged by serving underrepresented students and volunteering in their communities.
- As school leaders, the participants felt a need to protect students through condemning all forms of stereotypes, discrimination, racism, and bigotry.
- The experiences of the participants had led to recognizing the responsibility of creating some sort of forum or Muslim principal group composed of other principals who share similar challenges or experiences.

Chapter Nine

Implications for the
Future and Conclusion

As one of the first endeavors toward the study of American Muslim principals
in public schools, it is hoped that studies in this field continue to be pursued.

Chapters 5 through 8 discussed the findings in depth with participant interview excerpts to illustrate the themes generated in this study from the interview questions and follow-up interview questions. Below are summaries of
the findings that align with the research questions to provide the best understanding of this subject matter. This chapter will also delve into implications
derived from this study that may assist in future studies.

ADDRESSING OF THE RESEARCH QUESTIONS

Prior to offering practical implications of the findings for educators, a final
analysis of the five research questions will be addressed for the purpose of
offering a comprehensive study of the subject matter.

How is the performance of American Muslim principals affected by their
religion?

The findings of this study indicate that Muslim religious identity plays a
significant role in the job performance of principals in public schools and
that American Muslim principals are often highly conscious of their Muslim
identity. As a result of the predominantly negative portrayal of Muslims and
Islam in the political discourse and media, American Muslims are continuously forced to recognize their status as the "Other," and Muslim principals

understand that as a result, school community members could view them as problematic or as a threat.

Therefore, American Muslim principals are extremely cautious in how they conduct themselves verbally and physically and believe that political correctness is vital to their performance and survival as a principal. Participants noted that Muslim principals have to "think twice before saying something," as anything that they express has the potential to be misconstrued.

All participants expressed that based on their Muslim identity and religious values, they felt a strong sense of responsibility to clear up any misconceptions or stereotypes about minority groups. This belief also extended to misconceptions other than their own that may be expressed in the school environment. As part of a minority group, these American Muslim participants understood the issues of other minority groups and empathized with them.

The notion of social responsibility underlies their drive to teach tolerance, respect, and embracement of diversity as well as civic engagement. Thus, they are inclined to support and promote educational programs and activities that foster community involvement and service.

How do American Muslim principals perceive their treatment as compared to that of their non-Muslim colleagues in their district, in their relations with their staff, students, parents, and their school community at large?

The media's presenting Muslims as an inferior group leads to the general treatment of Muslims with a sense of harshness and constant suspicion. In regard to this study, it certainly leads to the potential for American Muslim principals being treated more harshly than their non-Muslim colleagues. In some cases, their religious identity is used by others to create conflict or to make accusations such as their wanting to impose Islam on the school community.

Female American Muslim principals felt that they were treated differently from their non-Muslim colleagues and school parents, especially if they wore a hijab. In regard to teacher–parent interactions, some female participants stated that they thought that the hijab was a distraction, as it made parents cautious about approaching the principal. One of the primary reasons for parents having such caution stemmed from the misconception that a woman wearing a hijab is less educated and has communication issues. Thus, women saw the wearing of the hijab as a hindrance to the principal's relationship with the school community.

The American Muslim principals in this study felt that they were being scrutinized and as such, felt a strong need to prove themselves to their colleagues and community. One of the ways in which they did this was to maintain political correctness.

How do American Muslim principals perceive that non-Muslims view them?

American Muslim principals believe that most non-Muslims view them in a negative manner, as the "Other," and many participants related experiences of being made to feel inferior and foreign. Most participants felt that this was partially due to people being uneducated about Islam and not knowing Muslim individuals. Several participants indicated that colleagues sometimes held stereotypical misconceptions of Muslims, especially of Muslim women. The female participants stated that they felt that their leadership positions defied people's stereotypical misconceptions of Muslim women, which often relate to subjugation, lack of education, and being nonvocal.

Some participants mentioned positive encounters with colleagues and other individuals. Nevertheless, they recognized that others saw them as having a different and foreign identity. The acknowledgment of the difference in identity was not always a negative notion; however, in some cases, the defining of an individual as the "Other" can sometimes lead to serious discrimination in the workplace and emotional and health issues.

How are the challenges that American Muslim principals face different from those of their non-Muslim colleagues?

As compared to their non-Muslim colleagues, American Muslim principals face certain challenges. Due to their being perceived as inferior and foreign, these principals are extremely aware of and cautious about their behavior for fear of its being misconstrued by colleagues or members of the community. American Muslim principals have internalized a great deal of fear, which affects their psyche and outlook and, in many cases, leads to high levels of stress and anxiety.

American Muslim principals are not defined and evaluated solely as a "principal." Members of the school community may view the individual as a *Muslim* principal, defining him or her by religion as well as professional role. In contrast, principals of other faiths generally are not defined by their religious identity. Muslim principals also must deal with the challenge of addressing their collective guilt, as previously discussed.

How is the spirituality of American Muslim principals affected by their leadership in a public school setting?

Most participants claimed to possess a strong spiritual outlook that was not affected by their role as a school principal. Nevertheless, some participants acknowledged that their job demands affected their practice; some participants missed their basic obligatory prayers, removed their hijab, did not attend the Jummah prayer, or simply were too busy for the voluntary spiritual practices to which they once devoted themselves. Despite a decline in certain spiritual practices, participants still stated that they felt at peace with God and with their practices related to their faith.

It became clear that one's spirituality can be vulnerable to the pressures as a public school principal. In some cases, the time commitment of the job may take away from time otherwise devoted to spiritual acts. In other cases, spiritual practices may be forgone or abandoned due to fear that others may perceive the individual to be an extremist or acting in conflict with his or her position as a school leader.

When the Muslim principals underwent traumatic experiences related to their religious identity or practice, it affected their spirituality through detracting from their positive spiritual outlook. Nevertheless, traumatic experiences also may lead to a strengthening of spiritual practices or outlook.

LIMITATIONS OF THE STUDY AND RECOMMENDATIONS FOR FUTURE RESEARCH

While this study was the first of its kind in tackling the subject of American Muslim principals in public schools, it still had some acknowledged limitations. First, there is a dearth of research on American Muslim school leaders who serve the U.S. public school sector, and as such, there was no research with which to compare the findings of this study. Second, it was not feasible to find an adequate number of school leaders of every racial and ethnic background representative of the Muslim diaspora or an equal representation of males and females. Therefore, the experiences of these participants may not be representative of all American Muslim public school leaders.

FUTURE RESEARCH STUDIES

It would be valuable to replicate this study in other major urban school districts, such as Chicago, Los Angeles, Atlanta, Miami, Houston, and Dearborn ("The Biggest Muslim Capitals," 2010). This would provide the opportunity to study American Muslim principals post-9/11 on a larger scale and to determine whether there are regional differences in the lived experiences of the participants. It also would be worthwhile to replicate this study with American Muslim assistant principals and teachers who serve in public education to determine whether the issues faced by Muslim principals also are experienced by other school staff.

It would also be useful to study how school community members treat female versus male Muslim principals. Such research could examine the lived experiences of participants, with an emphasis on issues pertaining to gender, such as males' attending the Jummah prayer or females' donning the hijab as well as differences between the genders in terms of religious identity and practice. Ultimately, such research could contribute to an understanding of how gender plays a role in the religious identity of Muslim principals.

On a more comparative level, studies should also be conducted examining the experience of Catholic, Jewish, and Muslim leaders in public schools. As several studies have indicated, Catholic and Jewish school leaders have faced a fair amount of adversity in their professional positions, thus it would be beneficial to study the experience in comparison to Muslim leaders to potentially find common trends or other revelations.

IMPLICATIONS FOR PRACTICE

The findings of this study can be used to inform best practices as they relate to American Muslim principals who serve in public schools and have implications for practice for universities, school districts and superintendents, and principals. Additionally, the study may also be useful from a general perspective for all teachers, irrespective of background. Educators may find benefit in reflecting on their job roles and duty to address misconceptions and political spectacle that could potentially undermine teaching, learning, and leading.

UNIVERSITY PRACTICES

First, it is critical for universities to recognize the need to conduct research on American Muslims. American Muslim educators, in particular, are a largely ignored minority in the education literature. Research can be used as a foundation to provide these educators with the support that they need and to encourage more American Muslim teachers and assistant principals to seek principalship. It is important that those who serve as principals reflect the diversity of the student body and of this country.

DISTRICT PRACTICES

School districts and superintendents should consider convening district-wide workshops focused on the concerns of Muslims in America to encourage understanding and dialogue among assistant principals and principals. Within the workshops, focus groups could be created in which common problems experienced in leadership positions and the support offered by the district can be discussed. Although these workshops would be oriented toward school leaders of all religious identities, the goal would be to raise awareness about Muslim principals, given the current political climate.

School districts and superintendents should identify or develop a curriculum that includes the study of Islam and Muslims in America, just as curricula are offered on other religious groups. Schools also could partner with organizations that conduct informational presentations on Islam and Muslims in America. Informational presentations would enable educators and students to have a better understanding of American Muslims and their "humanness."

SUPPORT ORGANIZATION FOR
AMERICAN MUSLIM PRINCIPALS

The creation of a national organization of American Muslim school principals and assistant principals is highly recommended. The main purpose of the organization would be to allow American Muslim school leaders to network, share their experiences with and support one another, and create a platform whereby leaders can exchange ideas and develop initiatives that can help strengthen their presence in the public education system. Such an organization would also provide mentorship opportunities, as experienced principals would offer advice to those with less experience.

AMERICAN MUSLIM ADVOCACY ORGANIZATION PRACTICES

Muslim-based organizations are also recommended to use this study to better understand the needs of American Muslims in the field of education. A large portion of the current discourse on Muslims and education centers around full-time Islamic schools and their needs. And while education forums that are organized by Muslim-based organizations exist, there is little assistance for public school teachers and leaders. This study should be used to inform the organizations and their audiences and masses. It is hoped that such information would lead to deeper understanding, the establishment of support systems, and organizational leadership for school leaders.

RELIGIOUS ACCOMMODATION POLICY

Finally, it is recommended that a policy that allows American Muslim school employees to attend religious services on Friday afternoons be established. As found in this study, male participants do not attend the religiously mandated Friday prayer service out of fear of losing their jobs. It is recommended that principals and teachers be provided with religious accommodations to attend Jummah prayer in lieu of taking a lunch period. Such a policy would strengthen the identity and confidence of American Muslim youth through the honoring of the observance of Muslim holidays. New York City and

Dearborn as well as some districts in New Jersey, Massachusetts, and Vermont already have such a policy (Botelho, 2015).

FINAL THOUGHTS

This book may be one of the first endeavors toward the study of American Muslim principals in public schools, but it is hoped that it provides a deep understanding of the current state and climate. Additionally, it is intended that this research motivates others to take on further studies and make efforts on catering to and improving the condition of minority principals in general. As stated in the previous and present chapters, to create identity support groups or organizations and catering policies to the needs of Muslim principals would hopefully contribute toward the betterment of their experiences in public schools.

References

Ali, W., Clifton, E., Duss, M., Fang, L., Keyes, S., & Shakir, F. (2011). Fear, Inc.: The roots of the Islamophobia network in America. *Center for American Progress.* Retrieved from https://www.americanprogress.org/issues/religion/report/2011/08/26/10165/fear-inc/

Ali, Y. (2012). Shariah and citizenship: How Islamophobia is creating a second-class citizenry in America. *California Law Review, 100*(4), 1027–1068.

Almontaser, D. (2012). Khalil Gibran International Academy: From dream to nightmare. In L. Arrastía & M. Hoffman (Eds.) *Starting up: Critical lessons from 10 new schools* (pp. 117–135). New York, NY: Teachers College Press.

Almontaser, D., & Nevel, D. (2011). Khalil Gibran International Academy: Racism and a campaign of resistance. *Monthly Review: An Independent Socialist Magazine, 63*(3), 46–57. Retrieved from http://monthlyreview.org/2011/07/01/khalil-gibran-international-academy/

Altheide, D. (2006). Terrorism and the politics of fear. *Cultural Studies, Critical Methodologies, 6*(4), 415–439. doi:10.1177/1532708605285733

Anderson, G. L. (2007). Media's impact on educational policies and practices: Political spectacle and social control. *Peabody Journal of Education, 82*(1), 103–120.

Aziz, S. (2012). The Muslim "veil" post-9/11: Rethinking women's rights and leadership. *Institute for Social Policy and Understanding.* Retrieved from http://www.ispu.org/pdfs/ISPU_Brief_AzizTerrMuslimVeil_1126_(1).pdf

Berger, R. J. (2010). Jewish Americans and the Holocaust. *Contexts: Understanding People in Their Social Worlds, 9*(1), 40–45.

The biggest Muslim capitals in America. (2010, August). *Daily Beast.* Retrieved from http://www.thedailybeast.com/articles/2010/08/11/the-biggest-muslim-capitals-in-america.html

Blakney, R. (1955). *The way of life: Lao-Tzu.* New York, NY: New American Library.

Bolman, L., & Deal, T. (2002). Leading with soul and spirit. *School Administrator, 59*(2), 21–26.

Botelho, G. (2015, March 4). New York City public schools to have Muslim holidays off. *CNN.* Retrieved from http://www.cnn.com/2015/03/04/us/new-york-muslim-school-holidays/

Bridge Initiative Team. (2015a, April 25). Islamophobia in the 2016 Elections. *Bridge Initiative.* Retrieved from http://bridge.georgetown.edu/islamophobia-and-the-2016-elections/

Bridge Initiative Team. (2015b, December 21). Islamophobia in 2015: The good, the bad, and the hopeful. *The Bridge Initiative.* Retrieved from http://bridge.georgetown.edu/islamophobia-in-2015-the-good-the-bad-and-the-hopeful/

Brooks, M. C. (2010). Religious conversion to Islam and its influence on workplace relationships in American and Egyptian schools: A case study. *Educational Policy, 24*(1), 83–109.

Brooks, M. C. (2014). How does a Muslim teacher fit? One teacher's journey into and out of the American public school system. *Religion & Education, 41*(1), 31–50.

Brumfield, B. (2015). All schools shut down in Augusta County, Virginia, over Islam homework. *CNN Wire.* Retrieved from http://www.cnn.com/2015/12/18/us/virginia-school-shut-islam-homework/

Burgess, J. A. (2012). *Tracing the finger of God: The role of wonders in Catholic spirituality in early America, 1634–1824* (Doctoral dissertation). Retrieved from ProQuest. (No. 1037995954)

Collins, C. (2006). *A history of New York City public school teachers, 1920–1980* (Doctoral dissertation). Retrieved from ProQuest. (No. 305257659)

Contrera, J. (2015). Lawyer reveals details of arrest of "clock kid" Ahmed, plans to file suit. *Washington Post.* Retrieved from https://www.washingtonpost.com/lifestyle/style/lawyer-reveals-new-details-of-arrest-of-clock-kid-ahmed-now-seeking-15-million-damages/2015/11/23/7589f682-91f5-11e5-a2d6-f57908580b1f_story.html

Council on American–Islamic Relations. (2013). *CAIR-CA survey: Almost half of Calif. Muslim students report bullying.* Retrieved from https://www.cair.com/press-center/press-releases/12296-cair-ca-survey-almost-half-of-calif-muslim-students-report-bullying.html

Council on American–Islamic Relations (2015, December 17). *Number of incidents targeting U.S. mosque in 2015 highest ever recorded* (CAIR Report). Retrieved from https://www.cair.com/press-center/press-releases/13313-mosques-targeted.html

Creighton, T. (1999). Spirituality and the principalship: Leadership for the new millennium. *International Electronic Journal for Leadership in Learning, 3*(11), 1–8.

Creswell, J. W. (2005). *Educational research: Planning, conducting, and evaluating quantitative and qualitative research* (2nd ed.). Upper Saddle River, NJ: Pearson.

Dalia, D. V. (2005). *School leadership and spirituality* (Doctoral dissertation). Retrieved from ProQuest. (No. 305376083)

Dantley, M. (2003). Purpose-driven leadership: The spiritual imperative to guiding schools beyond high-stakes testing and minimum proficiency. *Education and Urban Society, 35*(3), 273–291.

Davidson, L. (2011). Debbie Almontaser and the problematics of paranoid politics. *Arab Studies Quarterly, 33*(3/4), 168–178.

Davis, P. W. (2004). *An historical study of American Catholic education and the oral histories of archbishop elder high school teachers* (Doctoral dissertation). Retrieved from ProQuest. (No. 305201881)

Deak, M. (2015, December 19). *Hunterdon Central teacher claims she was fired because she is Muslim.* Retrieved from http://www.mycentraljersey.com/story/news/local/hunterdon-county/2015/12/17/hunterd-on-central-teacher-claims-she-fired-because-she-muslim/77476146/

Douglass, S. L., & Shaikh, M. A. (2004). Defining Islamic education: Differentiation and applications. *Current Issues in Comparative Education, 7*(1), 5–18.

Edelman, M. J. (1985). *The symbolic uses of politics of America.* Champaign, IL: University of Illinois Press.

Edelman, M. J. (1988). *Constructing the political spectacle.* Chicago, IL: University of Chicago Press.

Elliott, A. (2010, March 13). Bias is found in city's ouster of a principal. *New York Times,* p. A1.

Fairholm, G. W. (1997). *Capturing the heart of leadership: Spirituality and community in the new American workplace.* Westport, CT: Praeger.

Feed Their Legacy. (2015). *#FeedTheirLegacy.* Retrieved from http://www.feedtheirlegacy.com/

Foley, K. (2010). Not in our neighborhood: Managing opposition to Mosque. *Institute for Social Policy and Understanding.* Retrieved from http://www.ispu.org/pdfs/ISPU_Not_In_Our_Neighborhood_Kathleen_Foley.pdf

Frey, W. (2014). New projections point to a majority minority nation in 2044. *States News Service.* Retrieved from http://www.brookings.edu/blogs/the-avenue/posts/2014/12/12-majority-minority-nation-2044-frey

Gallup Center for Muslim Studies. (2010). In U.S., religious prejudice stronger against Muslims: 43% of Americans admit to feeling some prejudice toward followers of Islam. *Gallup.* Retrieved from http://www.gallup.com/poll/125312/religious-prejudice-stronger-against-muslims.aspx

Gooden, M. (2012). What does racism have to do with leadership? *Educational Foundations,* pp. 67–84.

Gottlieb, J. W. (2007). *Exploring wounding: The experiences of a Jewish educator* (Doctoral dissertation). Retrieved from ProQuest. (No. 304757150)

Graseck, P. (2005). Where's the ministry in administration? Attending to the souls of our schools. *Phi Delta Kappan, 86*(5), 373–378.

Gray, S. H. (2000). The spirituality of leadership. *Momentum, 31*(1), 16–18.

Greenhouse, S. (2010, September 23). Muslims report rising discrimination at work. *New York Times,* p. 1.

Haddad, Y. (1998). A century of Islam in America. *Hamdard Islamicus, 21*(4), 88–96.

Haddad, Y., Senzai, F., & Smith, J. (2009). *Educating the Muslims of America.* New York, NY: Oxford University Press.

Halvorsen, A. (2003, August). *Prayer, fear and focus on patriotism/diversity: Three elementary schools' responses to September 11, 2001.* Paper presented at the meeting of the American Sociological Association, Atlanta, GA.

Hilal, M. (2014). *"Too damn Muslim to be trusted": The war on terror and the Muslim American response* (Doctoral dissertation, American University). Retrieved from http://aladinrc.wrlc.org/bitstream/handle/1961/16817/Hilal_american_0008E_10652display.pdf?sequence=1

Hirschman, E., & Yates, D. (2012). *Jews and Muslims in British colonial America: A genealogical history.* Jefferson, NC: McFarland.

Ibrahim, D. (2010). The framing of Islam on network news following the September 11th attacks. *International Communication Gazette, 72*(1), 111–125.

Jones, R. P., Cox, D., Cooper, B., & Leinesch, R. (2015). Anxiety, nostalgia, and mistrust: Findings from the 2015 American values survey. *Public Religion Research Institute.* Retrieved from https://www.prri.org/wp-content/uploads/2015/11/PRRI-AVS-2015.pdf

Kanji, G. K. (2008). Leadership is prime: How do you measure leadership excellence? *Total Quality Management & Business Excellence, 19*(4), 417–427.

Kellner, D. (2003). September 11, spectacles of terror, and media manipulation: A critique of Jihadist and Bush media politics. *Logos, 2*(1), 86–102.

Kellner, D. (2009). Media spectacle and the 2008 presidential election. *Cultural Studies/Critical Methodologies, 9*(6), 707–716.

Kelman, S. L. (Ed.). (1992). *What we know about Jewish education: A handbook of today's research for tomorrow's Jewish education.* Los Angeles, CA: Torah Aura Productions.

Keval, F. (2012). *Moral imperative as a strategy for transformational leadership and sustainability: An autoethnography* (Doctoral dissertation, California State University, Sacramento). Retrieved from http://www.csus.edu/coe/academics/doctorate/research/dissertations/cohort-3/assets/keval-fawzia-moral-imperative.pdf

Keyes, M. W., Hanley-Maxwell, C., & Capper, C. A. (1999). "Spirituality? It's the core of my leadership": Empowering leadership in an inclusive elementary school. *Educational Administration Quarterly, 35*(2), 203–237.

Korac-Kakabadse, N., Kouzmin, A., & Kakabadse, A. (2002). Spirituality and leadership praxis. *Journal of Managerial Psychology, 17*(3), 165–182.

Koyama, J. P., & Bartlett, L. (2011). Bilingual education policy as political spectacle: Educating Latino immigrant youth in New York City. *International Journal of Bilingual Education and Bilingualism, 14*(2), 171–185.

Krogstad, J. M., & Fry, R. (2014). Dept. of Ed. projects public schools will be "majority-minority" this fall. *Pew Research Center, 18.* Retrieved from http://www.pewresearch.org/fact-tank/2014/08/18/u-s-public-schools-expected-to-be-majority-minority-starting-this-fall/

Lauten, E. (2015, December 10). Alabama KKK actively recruiting to "fight spread of Islam." *Alabama Today.* Retrieved from http://altoday.com/archives/7396-alabama-kkk-actively-recruiting-to-fight-the-spread-of-islam

Leithwood, K., Harris, A., & Hopkins, D. (2008). Seven strong claims about successful school leadership. *School Leadership & Management, 28*(1), 27–42.

Leonard, K. (2005). American Muslims and authority: Competing discourses in a non-Muslim state. *Journal of American Ethnic History, 25*(1), 5–30.

Lichtblau, E. (2015, December 18). Crimes against Muslim Americans and mosques rise sharply. *New York Times*, p. A26.

Lubinsky, M. (1980). Jewish education in the 80's. *Religious Education, 75*(6), 654–658.

Malcolm, A. O. (2011). *Anti-Catholicism and the rise of protestant nationhood in North America, 1830–1871* (Doctoral dissertation). Retrieved from ProQuest. (No. 3472399)

Manseau, P. (2015, February 9). The Muslims of early America. *New York Times*, p. 17.

Mastracci, D. (2015). Stop asking all Muslims to condemn terror. *Huffington Post*. Retrieved from http://www.huffingtonpost.ca/davide-mastracci/muslims-collective-blame-terrorism_b_8583060.html

Miller-Kahn, L., & Smith, M. L. (2001). School choice polices in the political spectacle. *Education Policy Analysis Archives, 9*(50), 1–41.

Mogahed, D., & Chouhoud, Y. (2017). American Muslim poll 2017: Muslims at the crossroads. *Institute for Social Policy and Understanding*, 1–15.

Moore, J. R. (2009). Why religious education matters: The role of Islam in multicultural education. *Multicultural Perspectives, 11*(3), 139–145.

Moore, K. M. (2007). Muslims in the United States: Pluralism under exceptional circumstances. *Annals of the American Academy of Political and Social Science, 612*, 116–132.

Moustakas, C. E. (1994). *Phenomenological research methods*. Thousand Oaks, CA: Sage.

Muslim Advocates. (2011). *Losing liberty: The state of freedom ten years after the Patriot Act.* Retrieved from http://d3n8a8pro7vhmx.cloudfront.net/muslimadvocates/pages/47/attachments/original/Losing_Liberty_The_State_of_Freedom_10_Years_After_the_PATRIOT_Act.pdf?1330650785

Nacos, B. L., & Torres-Reyna, O. (2002). *Muslim Americans in the news before and after 9/11.* Paper presented at the Restless Searchlight: Terrorism, Media, and Public Life, Harvard University, Boston, MA.

Newton, R. M. (2005). Learning to teach in the shadow of 9/11: A portrait of two Arab American preservice teachers. *Qualitative Inquiry, 11*(1), 81–94.

O'Gorman, R. T. (1985). The foundation of the US Catholic Church's educational mission and ministry. *Religious Education, 80*(1), 101–122.

Peterson, K. D., & Deal, T. E. (1998). How leaders influence the culture of schools. *Educational leadership, 56*, 28–31.

Phan, T., Hardesty, L., & Hug, J. (2014). *Academic libraries: 2012* (NCES 2014-038). Washington, DC: US Department of Education, National Center for Education Statistics.

Rashid, H. M., & Muhammad, Z. (1992). The Sister Clara Muhammad schools: Pioneers in the development of Islamic education in America. *Journal of Negro Education, 61*(2), 178–185. doi:10.2307/2295414

Redick, A., Reyna, I., Schaffer, C., & Toomey, D. (2014). Four-factor model for effective project leadership competency. *Journal of IT and Economic Development, 5*(1), 21–35.

Robertson, J. (2008). *Spirituality among public school principals and its relationship to job satisfaction and resiliency* (Doctoral dissertation). Retrieved from ProQuest. (No. 3323771)

Robinson, M. B. (2011). *Media coverage of crime and criminal justice*. Durham, NC: Carolina Academic Press.

Sachar, H. M. (1992). *A history of the Jews in America*. New York, NY: Knopf.

Sahib, H. A. (1995). The Nation of Islam. *Contributions in Black Studies, 13*, Article 3. Retrieved from http://scholarworks.umass.edu/cibs/vol13/iss1/3

Sanchez, J., Thornton, B., & Usinger, J. (2009). Increasing the ranks of minority principals. *Educational Leadership, 67*(2). Retrieved from http://www.ascd.org/publications/educational-leadership/oct09/vol67/num02/Increasing-the-Ranks-of-Minority-Principals.aspx

Schiller, B. (2011). US slavery's diaspora: Black Atlantic history at the crossroads of "race," enslavement, and colonisation. *Slavery and Abolition: A Journal of Slave and Post-Slave Studies, 32*(1), 199–212.

Shah, S. (2006). Educational leadership: An Islamic perspective. *British Educational Research Journal, 32*(3), 363–385.

Shaheen, J. G. (2001). *Reel bad Arabs: How Hollywood vilifies a people.* New York, NY: Olive Branch Press.

Sides, J., & Gross, K. (2015). Stereotypes of Muslims and support for the war on terror. *Journal of Politics.* Retrieved from http://home.gwu.edu/~jsides/muslims.pdf

Stanwood, O. C. (2005). *Creating the common enemy: Catholics, Indians, and the politics of fear in imperial North America, 1678–1700* (Doctoral dissertation). Retrieved from ProQuest. (No. 305404774)

Starratt, R. (2005). Responsible leadership. *Educational Forum, 69*(2), 124–133.

Stewart, K. (2004). The exceptional leader: Creating a positive work environment through tone. *Women in Business, 56*(1), 31–32.

Takaki, R. T. (2008). *A different mirror: A history of multicultural America.* New York, NY: Back Bay Books/Little, Brown.

U.S. Conference of Catholic Bishops. (2015). *How we teach.* Retrieved from http://www.usccb.org/beliefs-and-teachings/how-we-teach/

Walker, A., & Riordan, G. (2010). Leading collective capacity in culturally diverse schools. *School Leadership & Management, 30*(1), 51–63.

Weaver, R. (2007). What principals need to know about ethics. *Principal.* Retrieved from https://www.naesp.org/resources/2/Principal/2007/M-Jp52.pdf

Weiner, M. F. (2006). *"They're our children, not yours!": Citizenship and group-based identity narratives in Jewish and African American multicultural movements challenging New York City public schools* (Doctoral dissertation). Retrieved from ProQuest. (No. 305311547)

Weiss, W. H. (2007). Effective leadership: What are the requisites? *Supervision, 68*(2), 18–21.

Wenger, B. (1996). *New York Jews and the Great Depression: Uncertain promise.* New Haven, CT: Yale University Press.

Woods, G. G. (2007). The "bigger feeling": The importance of spiritual experience in educational leadership. *Educational Management Administration & Leadership, 35*(1), 135–155.

Wright, W. E. (2005). The political spectacle of Arizona's Proposition 203. *Educational Policy, 19*(5), 662–700.

Yacobi, D. (1998). Rethinking supplementary Jewish education: Establishing a specialization and a profession. *Journal of Jewish Education, 64*(3), 4–15.

Younis, M. (2009). *Muslim Americans exemplify diversity, potential.* Retrieved from http://www.gallup.com/poll/116260/muslim-americans-exemplify-diversity-potential.aspx.

Youniss, J., & Convey, J. (2000). Spiritual leadership and job satisfaction: A proposed conceptual framework. *Information Management and Business Review, 2*(6), 239–245.

Yusof, J. M., & Tahir, I. M. (2011). Spiritual leadership and job satisfaction: A proposed conceptual framework. *Information Management and Business Review, 2*(6), 239–245.

Index

Abu-Salha, Razan Mohammad, 91
Abu-Salha, Yusor Mohammad, 91
advocacy organizations, 98
African American Muslims: arriving
through slave trade, 24–25; first
University of Islam and, 33; impact of
9/11 on, 56–57, 65–66; Nation of Islam
and, 25–26, 33. *See also* Aziz (case
study)
African Americans: dehumanized as
justification for slave trade, 30;
demographics of principal candidates,
23, 37
aggressive pessimism, 10
Aiman (case study): abandoning prayers,
80–81; background, 44; on collective
guilt, 90; on media, 59; on nationalism,
66; on political climate, 57; on
spirituality, 84
Ali, Noble Drew, 25
Almontaser, Debbie, 37
Altheide, D., xviii
American Muslim community: challenges
of principals in, 95; demographics of
principal candidates, 23; diversity of,
xvii–xviii; migration and settlement of
immigrants, 26–27; prejudice
experienced by, 30–32; school leaders
in, xix–xx. *See also* African American
Muslims; Islam; Muslim American
experience

American Muslim school principals study:
background, xix–xx; best practices
from findings, 97; code of ethics, 48;
compliance issues, 42; data analysis,
47–48; data collection, 45–47; district-
wide practices, recommendations for,
97–98; future research possibilities,
96–97; interviews, 49; limitations of,
96; methodology, 40–41, 42, 43;
participants, 39, 40–41, 42, 43, 49;
privacy issues, 49; research questions,
1, 39, 49, 93–96; time frame for, 44–45.
See also Aiman (case study); Aziz (case
study); Najla (case study); political
spectacle; Rana (case study); Rula (case
study)
American Society of Muslims (ASM), 26
analytic autoethnographic study, 37
Anderson, G. L., 52
anti-Catholic sentiment, 10–11, 15–16, 19
anti-Muslim/anti-Islam sentiments: fear of
Islam, xii–xiii; mass media portrayals
and, xiii–xiv; post-9/11, xii, xiii–xiv;
during study time frame, 44–45
anti-Semitism, 12, 13
Arabic language, 67
ASM (American Society of Muslims), 26
author's experience, xx–xxi
Awful Disclosure (Monk), 16
Aziz (case study): background, 43; on
collective guilt, 90; discomfort talking

107

About the Author

Debbie Almontaser was the founding and former principal of the Khalil Gibran International Academy in Brooklyn, New York. A 25-year veteran of the NYC Public School System, she taught and served as a director in special education and inclusion, trained teachers in literacy, and served as a multicultural specialist and diversity advisor. She is the founder and CEO of Bridging Cultures Group, Inc., and a professor at the College of Staten Island's School of Education in the Post Masters Advanced Certificate Program for Leadership in Education.